LIBRARY MANUALS

Volume 7

LIBRARY CO-OPERATION IN THE BRITISH ISLES

LIBRARY CO-OPERATION IN THE BRITISH ISLES

LUXMOORE NEWCOMBE

LONDON AND NEW YORK

First published 1937 by George Allen & Unwin Ltd

This edition first published in 2022
by Routledge
4 Park Square, Milton Park, Abingdon, Oxon OX14 4RN

and by Routledge
605 Third Avenue, New York, NY 10017

Routledge is an imprint of the Taylor & Francis Group, an informa business

Copyright © 1937 by Taylor & Francis.

All rights reserved. No part of this book may be reprinted or reproduced or utilised in any form or by any electronic, mechanical, or other means, now known or hereafter invented, including photocopying and recording, or in any information storage or retrieval system, without permission in writing from the publishers.

Trademark notice: Product or corporate names may be trademarks or registered trademarks, and are used only for identification and explanation without intent to infringe.

British Library Cataloguing in Publication Data
A catalogue record for this book is available from the British Library

ISBN: 978-1-03-213109-2 (Set)
ISBN: 978-1-00-322771-7 (Set) (ebk)
ISBN: 978-1-03-213363-8 (Volume 7) (hbk)
ISBN: 978-1-03-213364-5 (Volume 7) (pbk)
ISBN: 978-1-00-322887-5 (Volume 7) (ebk)

DOI: 10.4324/9781003228875

Publisher's Note
The publisher has gone to great lengths to ensure the quality of this reprint but points out that some imperfections in the original copies may be apparent.

Disclaimer
The publisher has made every effort to trace copyright holders and would welcome correspondence from those they have been unable to trace.

LIBRARY CO-OPERATION
IN THE
BRITISH ISLES

by

LUXMOORE NEWCOMBE

*Principal Executive Officer and Librarian,
The National Central Library; formerly
Librarian of University College,
London*

LONDON
GEORGE ALLEN & UNWIN LTD
MUSEUM STREET

FIRST PUBLISHED IN 1937

All rights reserved
PRINTED IN GREAT BRITAIN BY
UNWIN BROTHERS LTD., WOKING

GENERAL INTRODUCTION TO THE SERIES

by W. E. DOUBLEDAY, HON. F.L.A.

THIS new Series of Handbooks is intended to supplement the larger Manuals issued by Messrs. Allen & Unwin and the Library Association under the title of *The Library Association Series of Library Manuals*.

There are some aspects of Library work which, although by no means unimportant, are of themselves insufficient to require a full-sized manual, and there are other phases which in a comprehensive textbook of manageable dimensions could be dealt with only in a general way. The Handbooks will adequately cover these subjects and will also treat of certain special topics which hitherto have escaped the attention which they deserve, or which—owing to recent developments—demand reconsideration.

Since Library practice must always be in accordance with the particular requirements of different types and sizes of Libraries, variant methods will be indicated from time to time, and a working basis for individual adoption and comparative study will thus be provided. University, Municipal, School, and Special Libraries —rural as well as urban—will be comprehended within the scope of the Practical Library Handbooks, and in each instance the latest advances will be described.

This smaller Series is issued independently by Messrs. George Allen & Unwin Ltd., and the range is sufficiently wide to make the volumes appeal to Administrators, Librarians, Assistants, and Students who intend to sit at the professional examinations. It is hoped that they will be of great practical assistance for immediate use in enhancing and forwarding still further that improvement in Library service which has been so marked since the passing of the Public Libraries Act of 1919.

To
JOAN

ACKNOWLEDGMENT

MY sincere thanks are offered to Mr. J. H. P. Pafford for so patiently reading the manuscript of this book and for many helpful suggestions. My thanks are due also to Mr. W. E. Doubleday for a similar much appreciated service. I am grateful also for the kind assistance so readily given by a number of librarians to whom requests for information have been sent.

L. N.

CONTENTS

		PAGE
	GENERAL INTRODUCTION	9
	ACKNOWLEDGMENT	12

CHAPTER

I.	THE NEED FOR AN ORGANIZED SYSTEM OF LIBRARY CO-OPERATION	17
II.	THE FOUNDATION AND DEVELOPMENT OF LIBRARY CO-OPERATION IN THE BRITISH ISLES	30
III.	THE NATIONAL CENTRAL LIBRARY: ITS ORIGIN AND DEVELOPMENT	50
IV.	THE NATIONAL CENTRAL LIBRARY AND ITS PLACE IN THE NATIONAL SYSTEM	60
V.	THE OUTLIER LIBRARIES, AND THE SCOTTISH AND THE IRISH CENTRAL LIBRARIES FOR STUDENTS	75
VI.	THE REGIONAL LIBRARY SYSTEMS	83
VII.	THE UNIVERSITY LIBRARIES INTER-LENDING SYSTEM	104
VIII.	INTERNATIONAL LIBRARY LOANS	107
IX.	UNION CATALOGUES	112

X.	HOW IT ALL WORKS	140
XI.	POSSIBLE FUTURE DEVELOPMENTS	143
	APPENDIX. PROCEDURE FOR BORROWING BOOKS THROUGH REGIONAL LIBRARY BUREAUX	149
	BIBLIOGRAPHY	155
	INDEX	179

LIST OF ILLUSTRATIONS

MAP OF THE REGIONAL LIBRARY SYSTEMS	*Frontispiece*
DESPATCHING BOOKS	*facing page* 48
A BOOK-STACK AT THE NATIONAL CENTRAL LIBRARY	*facing page* 64
AN APPLICATION FORM	*page* 68
A SECTION OF THE CARD CATALOGUE	*facing page* 80
A SECTION OF THE NATIONAL UNION CATALOGUE	*facing page* 96
A LONDON UNION CATALOGUE CARD	*page* 129
A REGIONAL UNION CATALOGUE SLIP	*page* 132

LIBRARY CO-OPERATION IN THE BRITISH ISLES

CHAPTER I

THE NEED FOR AN ORGANIZED SYSTEM OF LIBRARY CO-OPERATION

THERE is nothing new about the lending of books between one library and another. In the British Isles the practice goes back for half a century or more, during which librarians frequently asked their colleagues to lend books. But little was achieved in this way; partly because the would-be borrowing librarian often did not know in which library a copy of the book required was available, and partly because the regulations of many libraries were interpreted so strictly that the librarian did not dare to break them by sending a book outside his own town. At the best, it was a haphazard method—or lack of method—and depended largely upon the borrowing librarian being able to address his colleague as "Dear Smith" and not "Dear Sir." However, books *were* lent, and the practice of unofficial lending was growing steadily when the first suggestions were made for the introduction of an organized system of library co-operation.

In his letters on the "Reformed Librarie-Keeper"[1] John Durie wrote in 1650:

"The Librarie-Keeper's place and office in most countries are lookt upon, as Places of profit and gain, and so accordingly sought after and valued in that regard; and not in regard to the service which is to bee don by them. . . . But to speak in particular of Librarie-Keepers in most Universities that I know; nay indeed in all, their places are but Mercenarie, and their emploiment of little or no use further then to look to the books committed to their custodie, that they may not bee lost or embezeled by those that use them, and this is all."

But that was nearly three centuries ago. Now it is the aim of all—or nearly all—librarians to see that their otherwise idle books are made available to readers who may need them elsewhere. The day is gone—it is believed for ever—when all the books in a library, either university or public, are kept behind locked doors or barriers. There is a delightful story of a university librarian who, early in the nineteenth century, was seen crossing his college quad, looking unusually happy. His unwonted cheerfulness was noted by a professor who met him. On being asked for an explanation, the librarian, rubbing his hands with joy, replied, "All my books are in except two. Morley has those and I am on my way to fetch them!" That type of

[1] John Durie was Library-Keeper of the late King's Books at St. James's House under the Commonwealth. For an account and the text of his pamphlet the "Reformed Librarie-Keeper" see *The Library*, vol. 4, 1892, pp. 81–9.

NEED FOR AN ORGANIZED SYSTEM

librarian has passed on, and has been superseded by a new generation of men and women whose first aim is to see that their readers get the books they need. They are no longer content to say, "No, we have not the book," and leave it at that.

That being so, some method had to be introduced by which the librarian had a reasonable chance of obtaining the books he required. It was obvious that, however large his book fund might be, he could not—and in many cases should not—buy all the books for which he would from time to time be asked. This difficulty is not merely a financial one. Libraries ought not to buy all the books for which they are asked; but even if they should, many scarce books and back volumes of periodicals cannot be bought at any price, or, if a copy can be bought, it may take so long to trace that it is too late to be of use by the time it arrives. The librarian realized, therefore, that he must tap outside sources. It is thus that, starting with casual lending by and to friendly fellow librarians, the foundations were laid for the great national system of co-operation which is now making such rapid progress.

It is important to realize clearly what inter-library lending does and does not mean. It does *not* mean the right to expect—or even to ask for—the loan of such books as students' textbooks; cheap books which are in print, unless they are on a highly specialized subject; or popular books which the library can afford to buy for itself; and it does not mean that a library committee should use the privilege of being able to borrow books as a means of economizing in their own expenditure on books. It is, perhaps, natural that those who have had little experience in co-operation among libraries should fear that the possibility of being able to borrow a book instead of buying it might be abused. The experience of the National Central Library, however, is that almost without exception libraries play the game in this respect. If they do not, the remedy is in the hands of the regional bureaux or the National Central Library, which can refuse to deal with unreasonable requests.

What inter-library lending *does* mean is: (1) that many thousands of idle books are mobilized for service where they are needed; (2) that the money saved on the purchase of books for which the local demand must necessarily be small can be spent on books in frequent demand; (3) that the National Central Library is not called upon to buy books which are lying idle elsewhere—often a few miles from the library requiring them. The Central Library is thus able to buy other books, many of which could not otherwise be bought out of its limited book fund; and (4) that a librarian is able to say that he can supply almost any book for which there is a genuine need.

It has sometimes been suggested that there is a danger that the establishment of the National Central Library and the regional systems may make it difficult for publishers to issue scholarly works of an expensive nature; but there is reason to believe that the contrary is likely to be the case. It is known that in many cases the fact that a book has been borrowed from another library has led to a copy being bought by the borrowing library because the attention of the librarian has thus been called to the importance of adding the book to his own shelves. It must also be borne in mind that library co-operation is intended primarily for the inter-lending of such items as out-of-print books, foreign books, and back volumes of periodicals, and that such new books as are lent are mostly of the type which the borrowing library could not afford to buy for itself. One of the rules for borrowing books through the regional systems reads:

"When a library has to borrow the same book frequently, it is expected that an endeavour will be made by the borrowing library to purchase a copy for its own stock."

The limited experience at present available tends to show that many such books are purchased. Any library which attempted to take advantage of its regional system to economize in book expenditure would be excluded from the system by the regional committee. Perhaps the greatest safeguard of all is the steady but marked increase in the number of "scholarly" books asked for at the public libraries: an increase due to a large extent to the knowledge that such books can now be obtained through the regional bureaux and the National Central Library. This increased demand is leading to the sale of many additional copies to libraries which were at one time rarely asked for such books.

A side of library co-operation which is liable to be overlooked, but which is of great importance, is that the introduction of the regional systems has brought together library authorities and librarians as nothing else has before. This has been a great help to library authorities. But it is in bringing the librarians together that the regional systems have rendered so great a service. They have broken down the barrier that sometimes stood between the municipal librarian and the county librarian, or, to a greater extent, between the municipal librarian and the university or special librarian; a purely imaginary barrier which did not really exist, but which was doing an immense amount of harm, not only to the librarians themselves but to the full development of the library service of the country. Librarians now serve on the same committees, where they find that the other fellow is not such a bad sort after all, and that he is doing much the same work as they are and has the interests of his readers at heart just as they have. As Mr. C. Nowell said at the Library Association Conference in 1935: "The parochial boundary has largely ceased to function in the modern library world; librarians are no longer keepers, but distributors of books."

So, putting on one side the tremendous service in bringing books to readers and in popularizing the use of books, the regional systems have served a most important purpose in bringing library authorities and librarians together in a way that is bound to benefit the library movement in years to come.

The value—even the necessity—of use normally being made of the recognized regional or national centre must be stressed. The primary object of co-operation is to provide a service which will enable a reader to obtain a book to which he would otherwise not have access. When a librarian knows, or thinks he knows, where a wanted book is, there may be a temptation to follow the apparently easy course of getting into direct touch with the librarian possessing a copy. But there are good reasons why this method should not be adopted, except in unusually urgent cases where it is known that a certain library has the book and is willing to lend it. Experience shows that this "short cut" often leads to delay. The fact that a library has lent a particular book before does not prove that it may be able to lend it again when wanted. It may be in the hands of another reader; it may have been lent to another library; it may be at the binders'; it may have been temporarily mislaid; it may have been discarded. Now that the large majority of libraries are taking their share in the national lending system, direct lending between one library and another prevents the even and fair distribution of lending among all libraries. This was illustrated by the early and un-organized inter-lending among some of the university libraries, under which two libraries with good and up-to-date printed catalogues did nearly all the lending, simply because the librarians of the borrowing libraries were able to locate the books in their catalogues, and were ignorant of the whereabouts of other copies. Now, both at the National Central Library and in nearly all the regional systems, every effort is made to distribute the lending among all libraries. With the growth of the union catalogues this is becoming easier.[1]

Two examples will illustrate the value of making use of the recognized channel for obtaining books. A Cambridge scholar could not complete a piece of research until he had seen a certain exceptionally rare book. He enquired for it at the Cambridge University Library, the Bodleian, the British Museum, and several other important libraries in the British Isles and on the Continent; but without success. The only copy he could trace was in one of the great libraries in America, so he decided to go there to see it. On opening the book in the American library he read a note on the fly-leaf stating that only one other copy of the book was known to exist and that was in the library of one of the Cambridge colleges. This proved to be the case. Had the scholar sent an inquiry through any library to the National Central Library, the Cambridge copy would in all probability have been traced for him in a week or two.

[1] See pages 119–121.

The second case is that of a man prominently associated with the League of Nations who wanted to borrow a scarce foreign book and wrote to the League of Nations Library at Geneva asking if they could lend him a copy. They replied that they had not a copy, but that one might be borrowed from the Library of the University of Geneva if application were made through the National Central Library. The reader then got into touch with the National Central Library, which at once obtained a copy from the library of a society less than three-quarters of a mile from the reader's home.

There are still some persons—though the number is decreasing rapidly—who fail to appreciate the value of their local public library, backed as it is by the national service. This failure is not confined to any particular class, and it is often made in areas where there is a thoroughly efficient library service. Such a person is making a great mistake in assuming that his local library will not contain any of the books he may want. Very often it does, if only he would take the trouble to find out; very often it does not. But the absence of the books is frequently due to the fact that such books are never asked for: if they were, they would be bought. To a large extent the character of the stock of any particular library depends upon the type of reader using that library. If it is used mainly by readers of light literature, its stock will consist largely of such books. If a sufficient percentage of the readers asks for books of a higher type, the library committee will be bound to meet that demand so far as their funds allow, and in most cases they will be only too glad to feel that the standard of the library's stock is being raised in this way. So by insisting that the reader uses his local library, the National Central Library and the regional systems are doing work of considerable educational value—educating the public to use, and by using improve, their library.

With the growth of the regional systems the applications received by the National Central Library become more "difficult," in the sense that a much larger percentage of scarce books is asked for. Many of these applications, even though giving author and title, necessitate a good deal of bibliographical checking before they can be identified and enquired for. Sometimes this is due to carelessness, but usually it is caused by ignorance of the exact title or the author's name, facts the local librarian is unable to verify owing to the lack of the necessary bibliographical tools. Some of the applications are easy to deal with—such as the frequent requests for Freud's books under the heading "Froid"—but others take longer to puzzle out. For instance it was not at once obvious that an application reading: "[*Author*] Hieman Husidity, [*Title*] Baur, [*Publisher*] Fischer and Lunz," was Baur, Fischer and Lenz's *Human Heredity*"; or that another application for Macgregor's *John Moffatt* was for The Gospel of St. John in "The Moffatt New Testament

Commentary Series." The names of authors and publishers are interchanged with surprising frequency, but are usually easily detected, as in the case of Woodward's *Primer of Money*, asked for as McGraw Hill's *Primer of Money*. Many books are, quite naturally and rightly, asked for by subject, neither the reader nor his librarian knowing the author or title of a suitable book.

Sometimes the applications help to cheer the staff of the National Central Library, as in the case of *In the Moscow Manner* asked for as "In a Moscow Manor," and *Religion of a Mature Mind* asked for as "Religion of an Amateur Mind." Another application was for Grout's *Burglary Risks* for the use of a gentleman temporarily residing in the county jail; while a prisoner in another jail wanted, through the local public library, "a book on locksmiths' work." A reader wanting a book on illuminated MSS. asked his librarian for Bell's *The Art of Illumination*, of which he had seen an entry in a publisher's list. He was most annoyed when he was given a copy of Bell's book, obtained from the National Central Library, and found that it dealt with the art of illumination by electric light. A book asked for as "D. E. Hall, *The Great Dane*" was identified as "J. M. Shaw, *The Great Dane*." There was a week's delay in tracing the book under the author's correct name, and in reply to a letter asking if Shaw's book was the one required, the local librarian wrote, "I shall be glad if you will cancel our request. The dog has died." Here is a quotation from a letter from a librarian complaining of the heavy cost of carriage on a book: "You were good enough to obtain for us the loan of the Elephants of Southern India, forwarded to us in a small wooden box per passenger train. The carriage was 5s. 6d., and there will, of course, be the return carriage."

In conclusion, it is well to remember that the future of the regional systems and the National Central Library rests in the hands of the library authorities and librarians of the country—who have so far been extraordinarily helpful and encouraging—as it is only by that full co-operation recommended by the Public Libraries Committee that we can hope for success. It is the duty—or, rather, one would say it is the privilege—of each one of us to enter into this spirit of co-operation to the fullest extent. It is only by our united efforts that the regional bureaux and the National Central Library will be able to provide that service which is to be expected from a great national system of co-operation. A great deal depends upon those serving in libraries in positions which bring them into touch with the reader who needs a book which is not on the shelves of the local library. Never say, "No, you cannot have it!" to a deserving reader until you have tried the vast resources at the back of your own—perhaps quite small—library.

Let us take to heart the warning given by the

Librarian of the Sorbonne in 1780, when he said, in his *Duties and Qualifications of a Librarian*:[1]

"The custodian of a literary deposit should especially guard himself against that unfortunate disposition which would render him, like the dragon in the fable, jealous of the treasures entrusted to his keeping, and lead him to conceal from the inspection of the public riches which had been brought together solely with the view of being placed at its disposition. What, moreover, would be the object of these precious collections, gathered at so great expense by fortune or by science, if they were not consecrated, according to the intention of their generous founders, to the advancement, the glory, and the perfection of science and literature?"

---

[1] J. B. Cotton des Houssayes. *Discourse on the Duties and Qualifications of a Librarian*, 1780. Reprinted in J. C. Dana and H. W. Kent's *Literature of Libraries in the Seventeenth and Eighteenth Centuries*, 1906.

CHAPTER II

THE FOUNDATION AND DEVELOPMENT OF LIBRARY CO-OPERATION IN THE BRITISH ISLES

IN this, the first book on library co-operation in the British Isles, it may not be out of place to make a brief reference to early suggestions and attempts to establish some means whereby books might easily be lent between one library and another. Indeed such reference is necessary if credit is to be given to the pioneers of one of the greatest movements in the history of the British library service. It is so easy to forget those who have prepared the way which has made progress possible.

A particularly interesting account of early attempts to establish a system of co-operation between Oxford libraries is given in S. Gibson's article, "Library Co-operation in Oxford,"[1] in which he says:

"In 1652, Dr. Langbaine, Provost of Queen's, wrote to Selden: 'I have engaged a matter of a score of our ablest men in that kind, to undertake a thorough survey of our Publick Library [that is the University Library], intending to make a perfect Catalogue of all the books according to their severall subjects in severall kinds: and when that's done to incorporate in it all the Authors in any of our

[1] Bibliography, No. 88.

FOUNDATION AND DEVELOPMENT 31

private College libraries, which are wanting in the publick, so that he that desires to know, may see at one view, what we have upon any one subject.'

"The first official attempt to secure co-operation centres round a scheme for the compilation of lists of books in College libraries not in the Bodleian. . . . In 1794 the following request was circulated [by the Bodleian Curators] to every College: 'Whereas it is in contemplation to prepare a new Catalogue of the Books in the Bodleian Library, the Curators request that the different Colleges would make out or suffer to be made out a Catalogue of the Books in their several Libraries, not in the Bodleian, in order to make the same more complete, according to the intention announc'd at the end of the last printed Catalogue.' In December 1795 the Curators stated that they had received no such returns, and begged leave to renew their application. Their success was small. In 1801 they received lists from Baliol, Exeter, Jesus, and Magdalen, and a few years later from Oriel. Eighty years later Queen's presented a list of English books printed before 1600.

"The scheme was again revived during the University Commission of 1850. 'Friendly relations,' said one of the witnesses, 'might also be established between the Bodleian and the other public or otherwise permanent Libraries of Oxford. This might be effected by employing some person to compile a Catalogue of all the printed books existing in those Libraries which are not to be found in the Bodleian.' "

But it was not until 1929 that serious work was begun on a union catalogue of books published before 1641 in other Oxford libraries but not in the Bodleian.[1]

[1] See page 135.

In 1845 Sir Anthony Panizzi[1] issued a report to the Trustees of the British Museum in which he suggested that duplicate books might be lent from the Museum library. Although nothing came of his suggestion, and there is no evidence that it was ever considered by the Trustees, this section of Panizzi's report is of such interest that it deserves reprinting in full.

"APPENDIX I

On the Advantages and Disadvantages of Lending Books from Public Libraries

In considering this question, no account ought to be taken of the pecuniary losses that may be entailed on a library by the fair use of its books. It is assumed that proper precautions will be taken to guard against a total loss of a volume or of its value, and as for the occasional damage which may be caused by either wilfulness or gross neglect, it is presumed that by vigilant superintendence it may be of trifling importance.

The strongest objection against the system of lending is: that many students are deprived of the advantage of consulting works in the library whilst lent; and that a large number of students are thus put to great inconvenience for the accommodation of a few.

On the other hand, no one can deny that a student who has it in his power to peruse a work quietly in his own house at any time, can pursue his studies with greater advantage than when he is obliged to limit himself to the hours

[1] Panizzi was the first Principal Librarian of the Museum to organize our great national library in the form we now know it.

during which the Reading Rooms are open, and when he possibly may not be able to resort to them.

If a public library could lend books to students at their houses, without interfering with the persons who attend the Reading Room, the only well-grounded objection to this system would be removed. This could be done by the loans of books being limited to duplicates. Not that all books of which a duplicate copy occurs in the collection, should therefore be lent; but no book of which a duplicate was not in the library should, under any circumstances, be lent out of it. The lending collection might have formed a very considerable library, had not the system of selling duplicates been followed since the foundation of the British Museum.

Under proper rules, and with this limitation, arrangements might be easily made for lending books out of the library of the British Museum, and give to English scholars the same advantages as are enjoyed by those on the continent, where the system of lending books from public libraries is universal. It ought to be well understood, that this accommodation is intended for students, not for idlers, and that the character of the bulk of the works to be lent would be of a different description, from that of the bulk of modern publications which can be obtained from a circulating library at a trifling cost.

The question is one of expense, and of expense only. The amount would be commensurate to the utility to which it might be wished to extend the principle. The larger the collection of duplicates, the greater its utility as well as expense: not of course for purchasing books only, but for officers, management, binding and space. But in proportion to its utility, a lending collection in the British Museum would cost less than a separate library for the purpose of lending only."

Dr. E. A. Bond, in his presidential address[1] at the annual conference of the Library Association in 1886, suggested that the more highly endowed public libraries should

"agree on each making a particular branch of literature or science a special subject for attention—each assisting the others to make their specialities as complete as possible." He recommended combined action in the purchase of valuable collections offered for sale. "The spirit of co-operation," continued Dr. Bond, "might be further carried out by a system of interchange of books and manuscripts on loan for the convenience of students, so that in forming its speciality a library would be contributing to a great general collection for the use of all."

In March 1902 Professor Sidney Webb read a paper before the Library Association on "The library service of London: its co-ordination, development and education."[2] In this paper he pointed out that, outside the British Museum, London had, in its public and other libraries, more than 200 collections of considerable importance.

"How is this vast library service organized?" he asked. "The answer is that it is not organized at all. Each of the 200 libraries hugs its own stores, has its own more or less imperfect catalogue on its own particular system, knows nothing of what exists outside its own shelves, accretes its own accessions in its own individual way, decides on its own purchases without regard to what other libraries

---

[1] *The Library Chronicle*, vol. 4, 1887, p. 4.
[2] Bibliography, No. 40.

FOUNDATION AND DEVELOPMENT 35

may be acquiring, and—so far as I can learn—makes not the slightest pretence at regarding its own particular collection as merely one item in London's vast library service, which cannot, without organization, attain its maximum efficiency. The library service of a great city can and surely ought to be something more than a couple of hundred almost accidental heaps of miscellaneous volumes, each maintained and managed in jealous isolation from the rest, and limited in its public utility by the lack of communication between the heaps—even, usually, by a dense ignorance in those in charge of each heap as to what may be hidden in every other heap."

Professor Webb pleaded for "a combined catalogue at a central office" in order that, in the event of a book not being available in his own library, a reader might be able to find out where in London a copy might be seen. He went on to suggest that "it would be possible to publish from time to time from careful study of the combined catalogue, intelligent lists of additional books needed by London as a whole. Librarians could then avoid purchasing books of reference already adequately provided elsewhere."

Twenty seven years later work was begun on the Union Catalogue of the London Borough Libraries, described on pages 125 to 130.

At a meeting of the Library Assistants' Association in April 1907, Mr. S. Kirby, of the Hornsey Public Library, read a paper entitled "Co-operation: a suggestion"[1] in which he said that it was a recognized fact that there were many books published which quite a large number of libraries could not afford to

[1] Bibliography, No. 6.

purchase. The most important step towards co-operation yet advocated was that each library should specialize in some particular subject, and, in connection with this, it was urged that by a system of interchanging books libraries would not only have at their command an immense collection of books but would economize. He suggested the establishment of a few large "store" or "central" libraries in different parts of the country which would provide the class of books he had described. These central libraries would have no direct dealing with the public: the books would be borrowed by library authorities only, and through them they would reach the public. The central libraries should be provided with complete author, title, and classified catalogues. The cost of these centres might be defrayed by the state, or, as an alternative, by a levy upon each library in proportion to the income.

In 1906 Mr. J. McKillop read a paper before the Library Association Conference "On the present position of London Municipal Libraries, with suggestions for increasing their efficiency,"[1] in which he suggested that the Education Committee of the London County Council should establish a central library for the provision of expensive books for students.

"It is suggested," said Mr. McKillop, "that the contents of the Council's collection should be lent on application to the public libraries and the libraries of educational

[1] Bibliography, No. 83.

FOUNDATION AND DEVELOPMENT 37

institutions which could then lend them to their clients. This method would avoid the necessity for a very large staff. The central collection would have as borrowers merely the eighty-five libraries and branches already established, and those which may be added from time to time by the boroughs in the future, together with the fifty or so polytechnics, and such other of the institutions for higher education as may care to avail themselves of the facilities offered. . . . In commencing the formation of such a collection as is suggested, it would be well if the Council would enquire from local libraries and others if they possessed any works which would be more suitable for the central than the local library. Many of the latter already possess considerable quantities of works rarely used, but of great importance, which merely take up valuable shelf space and would be gladly deposited with, or perhaps presented to, a central library, where they would still be available to the readers of the local library when required. The saving in capital expenditure by reasonable action in this matter would be very considerable, and the relief to overcrowded local libraries greatly welcome."

The first organized system[1] of inter-library lending appears to have been that promoted in 1907 by Mr. A. J. Philip, librarian of Gravesend. Under this system, about twenty of the London public libraries exchanged their printed catalogues and agreed to lend one another books. Each library had a copy of the catalogue—so far as it was printed—of each of the other libraries.

---

[1] The author apologizes if he has missed any earlier system, but information on the subject has not been easy to obtain. He would welcome details of any earlier systems.

When a book was wanted it was looked up in some or all of the catalogues and the library possessing a copy was asked to lend it. Information is not now available as to the use made of the system, nor is it now clear when it ceased to function. The system depended upon printed catalogues, and probably the gradual substitution of card for printed catalogues—the result of the introduction of open-access—made it unworkable.

A note on this system appears in the November 1907 number of the *Library Association Record*,[1] in which it is stated that:

"The Woolwich, Gravesend and Erith Public Libraries have agreed to lend books (other than works of light literature) to properly accredited borrowers in neighbouring public libraries, on application through the librarians, on condition that the standing rules and regulations be observed, and that all costs of carriage and insurance be defrayed by such borrowers, and that each Public Libraries Committee issuing tickets to such borrowers be responsible for the safe return of the books, and for the collection of all the costs involved; the same privileges to be accorded under the same conditions to borrowers in the Woolwich, Gravesend and Erith Public Libraries. This is a measure which should receive the practical approval of all Library Committees in London and the adjoining districts. It is a step in the direction of so correlating the libraries of the Metropolis that they may be treated by borrowers as one, and that a man who is a reader in Kingston-on-Thames may have free access to the books in the libraries of Islington

[1] *Library Association Record*, vol. 9, 1907, p. 600.

or Croydon. An objection which may perhaps be raised is that the balance of advantage would rest with the smaller and poorer libraries. This, however, would not be the case, as the larger libraries naturally have a more numerous body of readers, and would consequently be likely to make larger demands outside. Many of the smaller libraries, furthermore, contain books, especially local books, not to be found in the larger libraries. Proof of this may be observed in a very casual comparison of the catalogues of a small and a larger library."

In September 1912 Mr. Philip again gave a lead to library co-operation in an article in *The Contemporary Review* entitled, "A reference library for London."[1] This article, published at a time when little or nothing was being done, is of special interest because it contains several suggestions which were later put into practice.

"Co-operation," Mr. Philip said, "is almost unknown amongst libraries of all kinds. Friendly assistance may not be lacking, but its manifestations are few and modest. . . . It is true that an insignificant scheme of co-operation exists amongst some of the public libraries in the vicinity of the Metropolis, involving some quarter of a million volumes; but what is that in view of the millions of books lying unread—not waiting to be burned, but looking for readers? . . . It has served, however, to keep alive the spirit of reform in this direction, to show unmistakably that co-operation is both desirable and possible; and now there are signs that the object lesson has not been wasted."

Mr. Philip went on to propose the establishment of a Central Reference Library and Clearing-house for London.

[1] Bibliography, No. 33.

"There is no doubt in the minds of students," he wrote, "that the *ultima thule* of library administration and co-operation will be when they can walk into their own local library in any part of the kingdom and ask for books from all quarters of the world with the full and certain knowledge that they will receive them."

He went on to outline a scheme of co-operation which would include the lending of books between one library and another and the compilation of a union catalogue.

The Contemporary Review for August 1913 contains an article by "Some London Librarians" on "Our Public Libraries."[1] In this article it is pointed out that no library can rank as a fully equipped research library in any branch of knowledge outside its local collections and a few subjects of special local interest. The authors recommended the establishment of a Central Loan Library from which books could be borrowed when required.

"In presenting this scheme for the endowment of literary research," they said, "we have intentionally refrained from entering into details as to the organization or location of the Central Library Authority. Its principal function will be that of a distributing agency—a library clearing office; and for this purpose it must possess a record of the contents of all contributory libraries. Its secondary function will be to co-ordinate the work of all libraries under its jurisdiction, while its immediate effect will be to provide equality of opportunity for research throughout Great Britain."

[1] Bibliography, No. 41.

In a paper entitled "Possible co-operation in reference library work,"[1] Mr. S. A. Pitt suggested, in 1913,

"that the Library Association should endeavour to arrange—with at least the principal British societies—for loans of their publications on payment of a small fee to cover expenses. . . . A further possible development of co-operation is a well-organized scheme for inter-loans between reference libraries. . . . In formulating a scheme, the principal difficulties to be overcome are: ascertaining the location of books; determining those which can be safely lent; the safe conveyance of loans; prevention of abuse; and financial considerations."

In October 1913 *The Library* contained an article by Dr. A. W. Pollard on "A national lending library for students," [2] strongly supporting the suggestions of "Some London Librarians." This article stated that

"an important step will have been taken towards the formation of a national loan collection as soon as any two or more universities or colleges agree to give each other a right of call in respect to their special collections, so that volumes not needed for the moment by any student in one library could be borrowed for a definite term for the use of a student in another. . . . There can be no reason why this system should not be carried as far in England as it has already been carried successfully in other countries. In order that it may be set on foot, however, the contents of all the participating libraries must be known, and this involves expense.

[1] Bibliography, No. 34.   [2] Ibid., No. 35.

"So far we have contemplated only a system of loans between libraries of the same class, each library continuing to house its entire stock. . . . But the housing of books is an expensive matter. . . . Books which are dead in the eyes of a particular class of reader need not be dead altogether, but at present there is no means of disposing of unusable stock save to sell or pulp it, to both of which there may be grave objections. If a book stack were built where land is cheap and books could be deposited there without any absolute surrender of ownership, but on terms permitting them to be lent to other libraries during the continuance of the deposit, overcrowding might be immensely relieved and the books in question given a new and much extended chance of usefulness. . . . The depository, to which we may now give the more dignified title the National Loan Collection, would exist not merely to house volumes rejected by its contributory libraries, but to buy books which at present no single English library can afford.

"Probably any advance will be by a series of small steps. . . . The first step, an arrangement between a few libraries for mutual loans, should be easily taken if the right persons can be got together in a room. The next step, the co-operative purchase of periodicals, in its earliest stage is a simple development of the first, a few librarians making special lists of periodicals to complement instead of duplicate each other, and then marking all those bought with this purpose as exchangeable. It is reasonable to hope that as soon as these two steps had been taken a petition to the Board of Education to quicken the process by means of a grant would not go unheeded. . . . What seems certain is that each of these steps would suggest new forms of co-operation, forms which many librarians would refuse to accept until they had gained experience,

FOUNDATION AND DEVELOPMENT

but which, after the experience had been gained, might seem safe and reasonable. Round the three points here emphasized, (i) mutual loans, (ii) co-operative purchasing, ultimately aided by subsidies specifically allocated for the purpose, (iii) gratuitous storage for not wanted books, without complete cessation of ownership, a body might be built up of much better proportions than we dare set out to sketch."

In January 1914 the Panizzi Club was founded,[1] its object being

"to provide opportunities for social intercourse between the senior officers of reference and research libraries and to promote all measures tending to their higher efficiency."

It was never the wish of the members—there were only seventy-two—that the Club's activities should be merely social. They aimed at doing something useful, and the first—as it proved, only—piece of work they put their hands to was the compilation of a Union List of Current Serials.[2] Under the leadership of Mr. E. Wyndham Hulme a small band of enthusiasts set to work on this great task. Many thousands of entries had been accumulated when the outbreak of war in August 1914 put an untimely end both to the Union List and the Club. Had the work continued, it would almost certainly have led to some measure of co-

---

[1] For an account of the founding of the Panizzi Club, see Bibliography, No. 36.
[2] For an account of the proposed Union List, see *The Panizzi Club News-Sheet*, May 1914.

operation in the inter-lending of periodicals between the libraries included in the list.

The July 1914 number of *The Library*[1] contained a paper read before the Panizzi Club the previous month by Dr. A. W. Pollard. In this paper Dr. Pollard deplored the absence of any kind of co-operative organization among the learned libraries of London.

"While it must be our business to promote co-operation," he said, "it is well to remember that the idea that a library can exist to be used by anyone except those who directly or indirectly pay to maintain it is one which needs to be put forward with great caution. The primary responsibility of every library is, of course, to its own particular body of readers, and if the slightest colour is lent to the idea that these may suffer from the librarian taking a wider view of his functions, plans for co-operation will be very seriously checked."

Dr. Pollard went on to suggest how co-operation might be introduced.

In 1917 the Birmingham and Coventry Libraries Committees, on the initiative of the Birmingham Committee, resolved:

"That the librarian be authorized to lend to other libraries, for a short period, books from the Reference Library which are difficult to obtain elsewhere, provided that under no circumstances shall books be lent which could not be replaced."

In a Memorandum[2] on this resolution Mr. E. A. Savage suggested that it would probably be desirable to organize

[1] Bibliography, No. 37.   [2] Ibid., No. 39.

FOUNDATION AND DEVELOPMENT 45

library exchange areas. "All the advantages of this organization," he said, "would not be on the side of the smaller libraries, even in inter-library lending, particularly if steps were taken to catalogue special collections."

Chapter 2 of Colonel J. M. Mitchell's *Report on Public Libraries*,[1] published in 1924, is a valuable contribution to the literature of library co-operation. The Report shows that at the date of its publication little was being done in the way of active co-operation.

"In general," Colonel Mitchell said, "it is fair to say that, while individual librarians in many places arrange privately for mutual loans, systematic co-operation is yet in its infancy.... The librarian of one of the Lancashire towns reports that an attempt has been made with two neighbouring towns to arrange that each shall specialize in one or more specific subject, interest in which is common to all three. Thus, assuming nucleus collections in all three, one specializes in cotton manufacture, another in engineering, another in paper-making. By means of exchange of catalogues, and telephone communication, readers in all three towns have reasonable access to three full collections which in the aggregate the three towns could not severally afford to buy.

"The difficulty of giving effect to a manifestly sound development like this is that of inducing library committees to abandon the parochial attitude of mind, and of securing an equally progressive spirit in several committees simultaneously and continuously. It would add to the efficiency of such an arrangement if there could be set up for each such group a joint book-buying committee, at the meetings

[1] Bibliography, No. 31.

of which all the librarians would be present. Except in the densely populated counties, the ideal unit would probably be the county, and the joint committee would include representatives of the county library scheme."

The Report referred to a suggestion "that the Central Library in Dunfermline [that is, the Scottish Central Library for Students] should have in its possession the catalogues of all public libraries in Scotland (the principle would apply in England, but it would mean a number of central libraries, each with its own district), and should be able to borrow books from any public library for the use of another. In other words, the Central Library itself would have a small stock, and act as a clearing-house for a mutual loan system. This suggestion . . . has in it the root principle of co-ordination between all public libraries, which is also at the root of the rural scheme."

In 1924 the Association of Special Libraries and Information Bureaux was founded. Although the lending of books is not the function of this Association, it yet forms an important link in the national system of library co-operation. The Association was responsible for the first—and so far only—complete guide to the library resources of Great Britain by issuing *The ASLIB Directory*[1] in 1928. "Aslib," as it is popularly called, brings together, in a way no other association does, those who administer libraries and those who use them. At its annual conferences librarians, research workers, university teachers, and the heads of industrial concerns meet to discuss common problems; to the great advantage of all concerned.

[1] Bibliography, No. 132.

FOUNDATION AND DEVELOPMENT 47

The Departmental Committee on Libraries in Northern Ireland recommended in their Report,[1] issued in 1929, the establishment of a State Library, which, among other things, would compile and maintain a catalogue of the books in all the libraries in Northern Ireland.[2] The Committee suggested that the principal function of this library

"should be to make good the deficiency in the provision for the securing and preservation of higher works; and that it should also be the centre of the co-operative system for the supply of books and of information on books and libraries. . . . We are satisfied," they continued, "that full use is not made . . . of the existing library facilities in Northern Ireland. We consider that the Ulster Library Committee should be charged with the duty of encouraging such use by the spreading of information, the publication of Select Lists and other bibliographical matter. . . . We attach great importance to the maintenance of relations between an organized library service for Northern Ireland and the service which is being developed in Great Britain, and that which may be developed in the Irish Free State, and we look forward to the time when the public and other libraries of Northern Ireland shall form a group in a federated library service for the whole realm."

The recommendations of the Committee have not yet been implemented: the reason being mainly a financial one.

If these early suggestions and attempts did not lead

[1] Bibliography, No. 28.
[2] There are thirty-three libraries in Northern Ireland; fifteen urban, five county, one university, and twelve special.

DESPATCHING PARCELS OF BOOKS FROM THE NATIONAL CENTRAL LIBRARY

to much being done at the time, they were not altogether fruitless: the seeds thus sown must have had some influence upon those responsible for the introduction of the schemes of co-operation which came into being a few years later.

This brings us to the end of the summary of the principal factors leading, directly or indirectly, to the establishment of the national system of library co-operation in the British Isles as it exists to-day. Before concluding, however, reference must be made to the great debt due to the Carnegie United Kingdom Trustees, without whose financial assistance, and broad vision and guidance, little could have been done. It is they who have taken the place of the State by providing the bulk of the money to enable the National Central Library to develop, they also who have financed the regional union catalogues, and it was with their assistance that the great group of special outlier libraries came into being and the work of the Joint Standing Committee on Library Co-operation was made possible. In direct and indirect grants to assist the work of the National Central Library the Carnegie Trustees have given or promised a total of no less than £244,000. Acknowledgment is due especially to the Chairman of the Trust, the Earl of Elgin and Kincardine; the Convener of the Trust's Library Committee, Mr. E. Salter Davies; and the Secretary, Colonel J. M. Mitchell, whose energy and enthusiasm in the cause of library co-operation have been boundless. Others whose names will always be associated with the introduction of library co-operation in the British Isles are Dr. Albert Mansbridge, as the founder of the Central Library for Students, out of which the National Central Library has grown; Sir Frederic G. Kenyon, the Chairman of the Departmental Committee on Public Libraries, who has given so much practical help; and Dr. A. W. Pollard, for all he did for the Central Library for Students as Honorary Librarian from 1917 to 1926, and in many other ways.

CHAPTER III

THE NATIONAL CENTRAL LIBRARY:
ITS ORIGIN AND DEVELOPMENT

IN 1919 the Adult Education Committee of the Ministry of Reconstruction issued their Third Interim Report,[1] dealing with libraries and museums. This report dealt at some length with the need for a State-aided "Central Circulating Library" and recommended that the Central Library for Students should be regarded as the nucleus of such a library.

"Such a library," the Committee stated, "is necessary in the first place to supplement the book collections of local libraries by supplying on loan local demands for larger and more expensive works than public libraries can provide, and for books of a more specialized character than local libraries are justified in obtaining. Even in the case of the large public libraries only one copy could be provided of such advanced and specialized works, and there is need of a reservoir from which further copies can be drawn in case of need."

The Committee went on to suggest that such a central library should organize the supply of bibliographical information. "We have insisted," they said, "in this report upon the importance of mobilizing the resources of libraries to ensure their maximum efficiency. . . . It could only be effectively carried out through a central organization which the Central Circulating Library should supply. The

[1] Bibliography, No. 54.

NATIONAL CENTRAL LIBRARY

existing libraries would be more fully used, unnecessary duplication of books would be avoided, and funds set free for fresh purchases. This proposal implies a general catalogue, which it would be the duty of a Central Circulating Library, acting as a clearing-house, to compile and keep up to date. . . . Such a Central Circulating Library as we have suggested would call for the co-operation of public, central, technical, and other libraries."

The particular interest of the Report of the Adult Education Committee is that, even as early as 1919, a State-aided central library, with which libraries of all types co-operated, assisted by a union catalogue and capable of supplying bibliographical information, was considered to be a matter of the first importance.

At their Annual Conference in 1919 the Library Association adopted the following resolution:

"That this annual conference of librarians and members of library committees records its agreement with the view expressed in the Third Interim Report of the Adult Education Committee as to the value of the Central Library for Students; suggests to public libraries the desirability of making an annual subscription to the Central Library; and strongly recommends a Government grant to the Library in order that it may fulfil the objects for which it was formed."

The Report of the Adult Education Committee did much to encourage the Committee of the Central Library for Students, who had already laid the foundation stone of a national system of co-operation. This Library had been founded in 1916 by Dr. Albert

Mansbridge, at the head of a group interested in the needs of adult students. Out of this Library grew the National Central Library. This is not the place to describe the work of that Library, as it is to-day: that is dealt with in other sections of this book and especially in Chapter IV. But the vital effect the establishment of the Central Library for Students has had upon the national system of co-operation as it exists to-day must be stressed.

The purpose of the Central Library for Students, as outlined in the First Annual Report of the Committee, was

"to ensure that all bona fide students coming under its notice shall be helped in their studies if they are unable to obtain the use of the necessary books elsewhere, but also to stimulate and develop higher study on the part of those, for the most part isolated students, who, owing to the lack of book facilities and book guidance, have been content with a lower level of knowledge than they are capable of acquiring."

The Report went on to say: "The development of the library will depend largely upon its relationship with existing libraries, whether serving the needs of educational institutions or the general public. Obviously it will need to be complementary and supplementary to such institutions. It will be complementary to big national libraries which do not send books out, or only to a restricted clientele. It will supplement the book supplies of libraries which are unable for various reasons to store a number of duplicates of books for which, owing to the development of local studies, there is a temporary demand. Its strength will to a great extent be derived from the fact that it will work in harmony with local libraries, and by so doing win their confidence and such support as they are able legitimately to give."

In October 1917 Dr. A. W. Pollard published an article on the Central Library for Students in *The Library Association Record*,[1] in which he outlined the work of the Library during its first year. He pointed out that, so far, the most common method of borrowing had been through the local centres of the Workers' Educational Association, but that

"it is desired to reach also individual students of all kinds, and in doing this the help of the local libraries of the districts in which the borrowers live may play a great part. . . . At present we are aiming at supplying the wants of students in the narrower sense of the word, we hope in the future to offer a basis for co-operation between libraries which shall enable us to be of use to those more advanced students who may already be teaching and writing on the subjects which they hope never to cease to study."

Dr. Pollard went on to say that "The whole spirit in which the Central Library is being worked is based on the idea that the library exists to be of use, and must be modified from time to time so as to be as useful as possible itself without interfering with the usefulness of any other institution, either now or in the future."

Soon after the publication of this article three public libraries began to use the Central Library for

[1] Bibliography, No. 51.

Students. During the first year they borrowed a total of twenty books. It may be of interest to note that the first library to take advantage of the service offered by the Central Library was the Westhoughton Public Library, which borrowed its first book in 1917. The honour of being the first library to subscribe to the funds of the Central Library belongs to Kendal Public Library, which gave a contribution of two guineas in April 1918. In the following month the West Hartlepool Public Library subscribed one guinea. Now almost every library in England and Wales makes a voluntary annual contribution. The other main sources of income are grants from His Majesty's Treasury, the Carnegie United Kingdom Trust, and other bodies.

In 1927 the Departmental Committee on Public Libraries, which had been sitting for two years under the Chairmanship of Sir Frederic Kenyon, issued their Report;[1] which was received favourably by library authorities. It is noteworthy that, with few important exceptions, the recommendations of this Committee had been adopted within a period of eight years, although not yet fully or always on the exact lines suggested. It is especially noteworthy that, with the exception of a small grant to the National Central Library, the State has not given any financial or other assistance in putting the recommendations into practice. This has been left to local authorities and voluntary bodies.

[1] Bibliography, No. 22.

"It is abundantly evident," the Committee stated, "that no library except a copyright library (and not always these) can become possessed of all the literature that an educated public needs. The great municipal libraries can meet most of the requirements of the general reader; they can do much for commerce, industry, and scholarship; but they cannot do all. The smaller urban libraries cannot even supply adequately the legitimate demands of the general public. The rural villages can only make a beginning. In all cases it is plain that, in greater or less degree, a library must be able to command resources beyond its own stock if it is to meet demands which will increase with the increasing development of education, and with the greater application of knowledge to all processes of commerce and industry.

"Briefly, our conclusion is that a national system should be built up on (i) voluntary co-operation, on financial terms varying according to the circumstances, between neighbouring libraries, whether they be county borough, municipal borough, urban district, or county; (ii) the grouping of public libraries round regional centres, which will generally be the great urban libraries; (iii) a federation of special libraries, pooling their resources in the service of research; (iv) acting as centre of the whole system, a Central Library."

Chief among the recommendations of the Departmental Committee were those relating to the establishment of a system of regional libraries and the expansion of the Central Library for Students into a national centre linking up the regional libraries. The third most important recommendation—the establishment of a central cataloguing agency—has not yet been implemented. The recommendations of the Committee in regard to regional libraries were not exactly on the lines on which the regional systems have developed, but there can be no doubt that the Report is largely responsible for the introduction of these systems. The Committee visualized a series of regional libraries around which all neighbouring libraries would be grouped. These regional libraries would be the existing large public libraries. The suggestion was that the regional libraries should act as a book pool upon which the smaller libraries in the area could draw. "The basis of such a federation," the Committee said, "would naturally be a payment made by the weaker libraries to the stronger."

The Committee recommended that "The Government should make an interim grant, which we suggest should be of the amount of £5,000 a year, in order to establish the existing Library on a sound basis as a national institution, and to provide for the extension of its work which is immediately necessary, and should set up without delay a Committee to work out the details of its transfer to the control of the Trustees of the British Museum.

"There is throughout the country an expectation that the work so well begun by the Central Library for Students will be extended as one result of the labour of this Committee. Many other reforms are desirable, but few can be carried out without considerable expenditure. Of all the feasible suggestions for increasing the benefits of the public library service, the extension of the work of the Central Library is the one which is immediately capable of realizing the most far-reaching advantages, and at a cost which, from a national point of view, is trifling. It is safe to say that no expenditure of a small sum would be likely to effect such an improvement in the general efficiency of the system, both in its direct advantage to readers and in its educational reactions, as an expenditure on the development of a Central Library administered on the principles suggested."

The recommendation of the Committee was that the grant should merely be an interim one payable for a year or two while the details of the permanent constitution of the Library—not, as it happened, under the control of the Trustees of the British Museum—were being worked out. It was assumed that the financial assistance from the State would ultimately be a considerably larger sum. When the payment of this interim grant was considered in the House of Commons[1] the Government shelved the question by referring it to the Royal Commission on National Museums and Galleries, which was then sitting. This action was a most unfortunate one, as it led to a body of eminent men having thrust upon them a matter entirely outside their original terms of reference, and a matter with which they were, as a body, not in touch. The result was that a recommendation which had received the most careful consideration of a body of experts, strengthened by the evidence of many witnesses with first-hand knowledge of the library needs of the country, was

[1] *Parliamentary Debates*, House of Commons, vol. 209, pp. 1147, 1154; vol. 211, pp. 694–5; vol. 217, pp. 1062, 1121–2, 1165–7.

overruled by a Commission of experts on an entirely different subject, necessarily lacking the knowledge of the members of the Departmental Committee and hearing no witnesses to support those of the Central Library for Students. The procedure adopted by the Government was most unfair, both to the Central Library and the Royal Commission.

The Royal Commission recommended in their Final Report[1] that the Central Library should receive an annual grant of £3,000 towards the cost of:

"(a) The supply of bibliographical information;
(b) The promotion of the Outlier system of libraries;
(c) The preparation of a union catalogue."

As a result of this recommendation the Library has been receiving an annual grant of £3,000 since April 1930. This grant was increased to £5,000 in April 1936. It is unfortunate that a sum of £5,000 should be the sole contribution from the State to the national lending library service.

On 21 April 1931 the Central Library for Students was reconstituted as the National Central Library; in the following year it was granted a Royal Charter; and in 1933 its splendid new building in Malet Place—the gift of the Carnegie United Kingdom Trust—was opened by His Majesty King George V. The full development of the work of the Library is now only prevented by the lack of an adequate State grant.

[1] Bibliography, No. 55.

In 1925 the Joint Standing Committee on Library Co-operation was founded by the Association of University Teachers. This Committee, composed partly of university teachers and partly of university librarians, under the Chairmanship of Professor F. E. Sandbach, established an Enquiry Office at Birmingham University for the purpose of arranging loans between the university libraries and a few special and foreign libraries. Most useful work was done by the Enquiry Office in tracing and making available books needed by scholars. But the Committee did almost equally valuable work as the first body to bring together, by means of its annual conferences, representatives of the university libraries. This contact has had many important results, the greatest being the compilation of a "Union Catalogue of the Periodical Publications in the University Libraries of the British Isles."[1] In October 1931 the Enquiry Office was transferred to the National Central Library. Details of the work now done for the university libraries are given in Chapter VII.

[1] Bibliography, No. 128.

CHAPTER IV

THE NATIONAL CENTRAL LIBRARY AND ITS
PLACE IN THE NATIONAL SYSTEM

IN considering library co-operation as it exists to-day in the British Isles it may be well to start with the centre on which so much of the rest of the system depends—the National Central Library.

The work of the National Central Library may be grouped roughly under three main heads: the lending of its own books; the tracing of books in other libraries and arranging for their loan; and the supply of books needed by students attending adult classes in England. The latter section is one of considerable importance, but as it has little connection with the subject of this book it may be dismissed with a brief statement that its object is to lend to students attending organized adult classes those books they cannot obtain from their local urban or county library or from the extra-mural library of their university. Books are issued in boxes for the period of the class session. This section of the work of the Library is organized as a special department, with its own stock of books, quite distinct from the general stock dealt with elsewhere in this chapter. The National Library of Wales does similar work for classes in Wales.

The first section, known as "The Library Department," performs to some extent the normal work of a library, though, as will be seen, its methods are far from normal. The Library is still a comparatively small one of about 140,000 volumes, but as soon as it is in the financial position to employ a more adequate staff it will be able to increase this number rapidly, largely by gifts from libraries. Fortunately there is accommodation in the building for a million volumes, so the difficulty of space is not likely to arise for many years.

Apart from dealing with books given to the Library, the chief function of the Library Department is to buy books—usually recent ones—not obtainable elsewhere. Books are bought each day as the need arises, but no book is bought until it is asked for by a library. When necessary a number of copies of the same book may be bought, the aim being to add a new copy when a fourth applicant is put on the "waiting-list." As books are normally issued for one month this means that a reader should not have to wait more than three months for a book in general demand. This rather long period applies only to the small proportion of books on the "waiting-list." Other books in the Library are sent off the day the application is received, or as soon as a copy can be bought.

The Library has certain rules as regards the type of book it does not buy or borrow from another library. These are of some importance and may be given in detail. Books which are considered outside the scope of the library are: (1) books which are in print published at less than eight shillings—if possible an out-of-print book will be supplied (unless ruled out under any other heading) whatever its published price may have been; (2) modern fiction; (3) modern poetry; (4) modern plays; (5) dictionaries, encyclopaedias, atlases, and other works of reference; (6) books required continuously for examination purposes, which should be treated as part of the normal cost of education; (7) handbooks which are part of the teacher's apparatus; (8) popular travel and biography of a journalistic type; (9) handbooks of sports and pastimes; (10) guidebooks; (11) music.

It might be thought that, buying books in the way it does to meet demands coming from all kinds and sizes of libraries, the stock of the National Central Library could be taken as a model one containing all the best books. This, however, is by no means the case, though most of the books bought undoubtedly come into the category of "best books." It may at first sight appear strange that the Library sometimes deliberately buys a second-rate, or even a third-rate, book on a subject while not possessing a copy of the best book or books. The explanation is simple and logical. A really good book on a subject of general interest, published at a reasonable price, should be, and probably is, in the reader's local library, whereas an inferior book on the same subject is not, the local library rightly not buying it. But to a research worker, or the person who knows his subject well, the inferior book may be of the first importance. Hence the duty of the National Central Library to provide a copy.

The other main section of the work of the Library is that known as the Information Department. This Department deals with those applications for books which cannot be met by the Library Department; that is, for those books which the Library is unable to supply from its own shelves. The first business of the Information Department is to find out where a copy of the book is and secondly, having located a copy, to arrange for its loan. With the friendly and helpful co-operation of almost every librarian in the British Isles the latter is by far the easier of the two tasks.

To set about its first task the Information Department first searches for the book in the various union catalogues. Details of these catalogues are given in Chapter IX. Search is also made in the printed catalogues of outlier and other libraries to which the Library has access. Should the book not be found, and should there be any outlier library in London likely to have it, a request is immediately made by telephone to that library. If these sources fail to locate a copy, details of the book are entered on one of the lists which are sent, in most cases twice a week, to various groups of libraries. The groups are (1) the regional bureaux; (2) the larger of the general outlier libraries;

ONE OF THE GANGWAYS IN A BOOK-STACK AT THE NATIONAL CENTRAL LIBRARY. THESE GANGWAYS, WITH A TOTAL LENGTH OF A MILE AND TWO-THIRDS, WILL EVENTUALLY GIVE ACCESS TO TWENTY-ONE MILES OF SHELVING

(3) the smaller of the general outlier libraries; (4) various groups of special outlier libraries, such as libraries specializing in (*a*) medicine, (*b*) agriculture, (*c*) science, (*d*) geography; and (5) the university libraries. This means that about twelve (often more according to the number of groups of special outlier libraries dealt with) different lists are sent each week, the average total number of books included in each list in the first three groups being forty-five. As a rule the same book does not appear on more than one list at a time. The object of this is to keep down as much as possible the number of entries to be checked by the staffs of dozens of libraries. Books are grouped by the National Central Library according to the libraries likely to possess them. For instance, if a book on agriculture is required it is put on a list sent, in the first instance, only to those outlier libraries specializing in agriculture. It often happens that eventually the same book may appear on several other lists; that is to say that if the first list fails to locate a copy the title is included on the next most likely list, and so on. This method naturally suggests a considerable waste of time. If every book were put on each list, copies, if existing at all, would be located at once. It would also be easier and quicker for the National Central Library to compile a single list and to check such a list on its return. The sole reason for not following what at first appears to be an obvious method is the difficulty of checking such a long list in the libraries

to which it would be sent. About 200 libraries, in addition to the regional bureaux, would have to check an average of 250 entries each week. Many of the smaller libraries would find this a task beyond the powers of their limited staff. Even if it were possible for all the libraries concerned to do the checking, the aggregate time spent on this work each week would be unreasonable—250 entries looked up in, say, 200 libraries, or a total of 50,000 separate checks, often necessitating a check in more than one alphabetical sequence. Even as it is, owing to the absence of a reasonably complete union catalogue, the aggregate time spent in checking the lists is considerable. The assistance given in this way is invaluable to the National Central Library, the authorities of which fully appreciate the work it represents.

When the regional union catalogues cover all the urban and county libraries as well as many of the university and special libraries, the number and length of the lists will be greatly reduced. This will lead to a considerable saving of time both in the co-operating libraries and the National Central Library.

When the copies of a list have been returned to the National Central Library, usually a few days after they have been sent out, they are checked on to a master-copy, which then shows which library or libraries—often more than one copy of a book may be offered—is willing to lend each book. Those books which no library is able to lend may go on a list to be sent to another group of libraries, or they may have to be given up and reported as unobtainable.

Each list is ruled into four columns: (1) for a running number for each book; (2) for the author, title, date and other necessary information about the book; (3) left blank when the list is sent out, but in which the checking library writes "yes" if prepared to lend the book for "Home Reading," and (4) for the word "yes" if prepared to lend it for use in a library only.

Having traced a loanable copy of a book the procedure for arranging for its loan is simple. If more than one copy is offered, the library asked to lend is the one which has (*a*) lent fewest books, or (*b*) borrowed most. This is an important service which can be rendered only by a central agency able to keep records of all transactions. It is only in this way that the lending can be distributed as evenly as possible among all the co-operating libraries. The National Central Library then sends a form to the librarian of the "lending library," asking him to send the book direct to the "borrowing library," or, in the case of a county library reader, direct to the reader's address.

When the book is sent, the "lending library" returns to the National Central Library a postcard (previously supplied by the National Central Library) saying that the book has been sent.

This completes the transaction, except for the entry on the appropriate "issue" card of a loan of one book to the "borrowing library." These issue cards are simple. At the top is the name of the library and below that is a space for the date and the number of books issued to the library on that date. Details of the books are not given, nor are they needed. Somewhat similar records are kept of books lent by libraries at the request of the National Central Library.

As the methods adopted by the National Central Library are necessarily different from those of any other library, a summary of the way in which a book is issued may be of some interest.

Applications for books must be made on one of the forms supplied to all libraries by the National Central Library. These forms are filled in by the librarian of the reader's local public, university, or other library. When the library is in a regional system the form is sent to the National Central Library through the regional bureau, as described on page 140. When a library is not in a regional system the form is sent direct to the National Central Library. The wording of the form, the original of which is 8 inches by 5 inches, is given on the next page. On receipt of the form—through the post—the Central Library stamps the date of receipt against the word "Received" in the third section at the foot of the form, which is then sent to the Library Department, unless it is seen that the book asked for is obviously one outside the scope of the Library—such as a novel, a dictionary, or a guide book—in which case a symbol indicating the reason for not supplying the book is at once entered

APPLICATION FORM					
From (*Name of Library*)					
To the NORTH WESTERN REGIONAL LIBRARY BUREAU, CENTRAL LIBRARY, ST. PETER'S SQUARE, MANCHESTER, 2.	Latest date (if known) on which the book will be of use				
Author (*block letters*)	Title			Date and edition of book	
A separate form must be used for each book					
Date	Signature of Librarian	Place of Publication		Publisher	Price
Name and address to which book is to be sent (*only to be given in case of County Libraries*)			If the book is of no use unless available for HOME READING the Librarian should initial this space		
FOR USE OF BUREAU Received Forwarded	FOR USE OF LENDING LIBRARY Received Waiting list Book sent Postage			FOR USE OF N.C.L. Received Acknowledged Waiting list Book ordered Book sent Reason not sent	

AN APPLICATION FORM USED FOR BORROWING BOOKS THROUGH THE REGIONAL LIBRARY SYSTEMS AND THE NATIONAL CENTRAL LIBRARY; SIZE OF ORIGINAL FORM IS 8 INS. BY 5 INS.

against the "Reason not sent" and a form giving this reason is sent to the librarian applying for the book. Once an application has been forwarded to the Central Library all communications are made directly to the borrowing librarian and not through the bureau.

The staff of the Library Department check the form with the catalogue of the books in the Library. If a copy of the book is on the shelves it is sent to the borrowing library, or in the case of a county library direct to the reader. The date is stamped against "Book sent" on the form, which is sent to the General Office to be dealt with in the way described on page 71. If the book is out, the library applying for it is put on the waiting-list, the date is stamped against "Waiting-list" on the form, and the library is told that the book will be sent as soon as it is available. In the case of a book on the waiting-list, the date is stamped against "Book sent" when the book is available. If a copy of the book is not in the Library one of two things is done:

(1) If it is an English or American book which is in print, and if it is unlikely that any other library would be willing to lend a copy (such as in the case of a book published quite recently), a copy is ordered, the date of ordering being stamped on the form against "Book ordered."
(2) If the book does not come under category (1) the form is sent to the Information Department.

In either case (1) or (2) the library is told what is being done and the date is stamped against "Acknowledged" on the form.

Books are ordered every day at the discretion of the librarian, the only limits being those of scope and the amount available for the purchase of books. All books are ordered on approval and any found, upon examination, to be unsuitable are returned to the bookseller.

Upon receipt of the application the Information Department look the book up in the various union catalogues and catalogues of outlier libraries, telephone to likely outlier libraries in London, and, if those sources fail, put the book on one or more of the "Lists" described on pages 63 to 66. If these and all other sources fail, the library is told that a copy cannot be obtained, and the date is stamped against "Reason not sent" on the form. Often, however, the application is sent back to the Library Department in order that the question of purchase may be reconsidered. The Library frequently buys books it fails to obtain through the regional bureaux or from the outlier libraries. A book of which no loanable copy can be traced should undoubtedly be in the central lending library. Many more such books should, and would, be bought if money were available.

So much for the issue of a book. It only remains to explain what happens to the application form and how a record of books on issue is kept, though there are many other things to be done in connection with the issue of a book through the post.

When the application forms have been dealt with by the Library Department or the Information Department they are sent to the General Office. In the case of a book supplied from the shelves or bought it is sent to the General Office with the form, where the necessary receipt form and address label are typed and the cost of postage noted. The application form is then filed, with those for all other books on issue, under the name of the author. These forms thus give a complete list of all books on issue; the forms themselves giving all the other necessary information—name of library having the book, date of issue, and the source from which the book has been obtained.

Forms for books which have been put on the waiting-list by the Library Department are filed, with other similar forms, under the name of the author, and at the same time a plain guide-card, on which is written the name of the author and the title of the book, is inserted in the "issue file" in front of the application form for the same book. The main purpose of these guides is to indicate to the assistant taking out a form for a returned book that another library is waiting for it: incidentally, they act as admirable guides to the issue file, as the authors' names are written on the tab of the guide card.

This may sound rather crude—and, indeed, it is—but it works well and saves a great deal of time. It will be noted that the borrowing librarian, when he fills up the application form, provides part of the necessary material for recording issues at the National Central Library, and the guides are kept for future use if required.

The receipt form, when returned by the borrowing librarian, is filed behind a guide card indicating the date on which the book is due back. This file is checked each day and, when necessary, "overdue notices" are sent. As there is sometimes delay in the return of the receipt, a carbon copy is filed behind a date card in another file until the signed copy is received.

When a book is returned, the application form is transferred from the issue file to a "returned book" file, where it is filed under the name of the borrowing library and kept for six months in case any query should be raised in connection with it. Another file —kept in the Library Department—contains the application forms, in alphabetical order of author, for books which have *not* been supplied. This file, which is kept permanently, is frequently consulted and often saves the time of going over the same ground again.

A section of the work of the Library which is, perhaps, little appreciated, simply because few persons realize that it is done, is the supply of bibliographical information. Every day many applications are received which necessitate a good deal of work before search for the book can be begun. Sometimes this is due to carelessness on the part of the person filling in the form. The author's name may be incorrectly spelt or even be quite wrong, and frequently the title is incorrect. This may not be the fault of the librarian making the application, who gives the information as he receives it and has no means of checking its accuracy. But the correction of these inaccuracies takes much time for which there is usually nothing to show. Other applications are for books giving information on a subject, or books of which the applicant can give only incomplete information. Sometimes he does not know the author or he is not sure of the title. Many of these applications are easy to deal with, but others necessitate long research at the British Museum or elsewhere. In particularly difficult cases the staff has the great advantage of access to the librarians of the special outlier libraries, who are experts in the literature of their own subject, and to experts at the British Museum and other Government libraries as well as to members of the teaching staff of some of the universities.

Among the books supplied by the Library are: (a) those needed by the general reader; (b) highly specialized or expensive books which the borrowing library would not be justified in buying, even if it could afford to do so; (c) scarce and out-of-print books, in some cases books of considerable age, rarity, and value; (d) foreign books, of which no copies are available in this country; (e) the back volumes of periodicals; and (f) photostat copies of manuscripts and rare printed books which cannot be lent. The monetary value of the books obtained through the Library would be represented by a very large sum each year, but the service should not be judged by this, but by its value to those who need books they would not be able to obtain in any other way. Almost every library in the country depends upon the National Central Library for those books which, for financial or other reasons, it is unable to supply from its own shelves.

CHAPTER V

THE OUTLIER LIBRARIES, AND THE SCOTTISH
AND THE IRISH CENTRAL LIBRARIES
FOR STUDENTS

REFERENCE has been made in the previous chapter to the outlier libraries associated with the National Central Library. An outlier library is one which undertakes to lend its books to other libraries through the agency of the National Central Library; that is to say, that in a sense the books in an outlier library form part of the national stock on which the National Central Library may draw. We thus find that the national centre has direct access to (*a*) the books on its own shelves, and (*b*) the books in the great group of outlier libraries. Indirect access is obtained to all libraries in the regional systems, the British university libraries, and foreign libraries.

The establishment of the outlier library system is due to the foresight of the Carnegie Trustees, who in 1922 made grants to the College of Nursing and to the Royal Aeronautical Society, on condition that the books in their libraries were made available to readers in all parts of the country through the Central Library for Students, as the National Central Library then was. This was done deliberately, and from that time onwards the Carnegie Trustees made a similar condition in connection with their grants to special libraries, to whom they gave, between 1922 and 1931, an aggregate of no less than £84,500. It is probable, however, that neither the Carnegie Trustees nor the Committee of the Central Library realized that the small grant made to the Library of the College of Nursing sowed the seed of a movement which, within a few years, was to be one of the greatest and most valuable systems of library co-operation in the world. At the end of 1936 there were 165 outlier libraries, containing no less than 6,570,000 volumes,[1] including some 32,000 sets of periodicals.

These figures in themselves are noteworthy, but their true value will only be appreciated if it is remembered that the list of outlier libraries includes, in addition to most of the great urban and county libraries in England and Wales, many special libraries containing the finest collection of books in the world on their own subject. The extent of the field covered by the special outlier libraries may be gathered from the following list of special outlier libraries from which books can be borrowed through the agency of the National Central Library:—

1. Irish Central Library for Students.
2. Scottish Central Library for Students.
3. Anglo-German Academic Bureau.
4. Animal Diseases Research Association, Edinburgh.
5. Association for Moral and Social Hygiene.

[1] Excluding fiction in the urban and county libraries.

THE OUTLIER LIBRARIES

6. British Boot, Shoe, and Allied Trades Research Association.
7. British Cast Iron Research Association, Birmingham.
8. British Cotton Industry Research Association, Manchester.
9. British Drama League.
10. British Institute of Adult Education.
11. British Launderers' Research Association.
12. British Leather Manufacturers' Research Association.
13. British Medical Association.
14. British Non-Ferrous Metals Research Association.
15. British Optical Association.
16. British Refractories Research Association.
17. Cambridge Philosophical Society.
18. College of Nursing.
19. College of Preceptors.
20. Co-operative Reference Library.
21. Courtauld Institute of Art.
22. Devon and Exeter Institution, Exeter.
23. Folk Lore Society.
24. French Hospital Library.
25. Geographical Association, Manchester.
26. Hannah Dairy Research Institute, Ayr.
27. Historical Association.
28. Horniman Museum.
29. Howard League for Penal Reform.
30. Imperial Institute of Entomology.
31. Institute of Sociology.
32. Jews' College.
33. King's College of Household and Social Science.
34. Lambeth Palace Library.
35. League of Nations Union.
36. Linen Industry Research Association, Belfast.
37. Linnean Society of London.

38. Literary and Philosophical Society, Newcastle-upon-Tyne.
39. Liverpool (Lyceum) Library.
40. London and National Society for Women's Service.
41. London County Council Education Library.
42. London School of Economics and Political Science.
43. London School of Hygiene and Tropical Medicine.
44. Management Library.
45. Manchester Library for Deaf Education.
46. Manchester Literary and Philosophical Society.
47. Medical Institution, Liverpool.
48. Meteorological Office Library.
49. National Book Council.
50. National Council for Maternity and Child Welfare.
51. National Federation of Iron and Steel Manufacturers.
52. National Institute of Industrial Psychology.
53. National Library of Wales, Aberystwyth.
54. National Operatic and Dramatic Association.
55. New Commonwealth Library.
56. Norfolk and Norwich Library, Norwich.
57. North Devon Athenaeum, Barnstaple.
58. Office of the High Commissioner for India.
59. Pharmaceutical Society of Great Britain.
60. Reform Club Library (pamphlet collection only).
61. Regent Advertising Club.
62. Research Association of British Flour Millers.
63. Research Association of British Paint, Colour, and Varnish Manufacturers.
64. Research Association of British Rubber Manufacturers, Croydon.
65. Rothamsted Experimental Station, Harpenden.
66. Rowett Research Institute, Aberdeen.
67. Royal Aeronautical Society.

THE OUTLIER LIBRARIES

68. Royal Anthropological Institute.
69. Royal Asiatic Society.
70. Royal College of Veterinary Surgeons.
71. Royal Dublin Society.
72. Royal Empire Society.
73. Royal Entomological Society of London.
74. Royal Horticultural Society.
75. Royal Institute of International Affairs.
76. Royal Irish Academy, Dublin.
77. Royal Microscopical Society.
78. Royal Scottish Geographical Society, Edinburgh.
79. Royal Scottish Society of Arts, Edinburgh.
80. St. Bride Foundation Libraries.
81. St. Thomas's Hospital Medical School.
82. School of Agriculture, Cambridge.
83. School of Oriental Studies.
84. School of Slavonic and East European Studies.
85. Science Library.
86. Scottish Marine Biological Association, Millport, Bute.
87. Selly Oak Colleges.
88. Societies for the Promotion of Hellenic and Roman Studies.
89. Society for Psychical Research.
90. Society for the Propagation of the Gospel in Foreign Parts.
91. Society of Antiquaries.
92. Society of Friends.
93. Solon Ceramic Library, Stoke-on-Trent.
94. South-Eastern Agriculture College, Wye.
95. Swedenborg Society.
96. Theosophical Society in England.
97. Warburg Institute.
98. Dr. Williams's Library.
99. Wool Industries Research Association, Leeds.

A SECTION OF THE CARD CATALOGUE AT THE NATIONAL CENTRAL LIBRARY

In addition to the ninety-nine special libraries, the outlier libraries include fifty-one urban libraries and fifteen county libraries. These two groups, although in the main general collections, are also of the greatest assistance, not only in lending the more general books, but also on account of the many valuable special collections they contain. Almost every library has a special collection of books of local interest—such as local topography and local industries—and many libraries have collections on other subjects also, sometimes large and sometimes small according to the nature of the subject. Often these special collections are of the first importance. There is, for instance, the great Shakespeare collection at the Birmingham Public Library, one of the most complete in the world; the Keats collection at the Hampstead Public Library; the Horace Walpole collection at the Stoke Newington Public Library; the Harsnett collection of fifteenth and sixteenth-century books at the Colchester Public Library; and the collections of Quaker books and of material relating to railway tracks at the Darlington Public Library.

In 1936–37 the outlier libraries lent 11,259 books. What were these books? Did they really matter very much? The answer is that each one was a book needed for a specific purpose by a person who could not otherwise have obtained a copy. All the books were scarce; some of them were unique copies so far as this country is concerned. Many were wanted by persons doing advanced research, and frequent letters of thanks and notices in the press show how fully this service is appreciated. The value of the service given by the outlier libraries is not limited to the books lent to other libraries, as a great deal of bibliographical and other information is given, particularly by the librarians of the special libraries, who are experts in the literature of their own subject.

With the establishment of the regional systems nearly all the urban and county libraries, and several university and special libraries, are now in effect outlier libraries; that is to say, that through the inter-regional lending system organized by the National Central Library they are willing to lend their books to any library in another regional system. In other words, they exclude only those few libraries which are not yet co-operating in a regional system. It is probable that before long almost every urban and county library in Great Britain will be in a regional system; thus being able to take its full share in the national library service. When this stage is reached the list of outlier libraries will include only those special libraries which are outside the regional systems. It will also, in all probability, be a much more comprehensive list containing the names of most of the special libraries not already included.

The list of special outlier libraries includes the names of the Scottish Central Library for Students and the Irish Central Library for Students. These two libraries are a good deal more than ordinary outlier libraries and their position in the national system should be understood.

Up to a point they act as the national central library for Scotland and Ireland respectively, but there are some important differences. They are financed entirely by the Carnegie Trustees, by whom they were established in 1923. So far as book purchase is concerned they work on similar lines to the National Central Library; the same type of book is bought and no book is bought until it is asked for. Libraries in Scotland and Ireland needing books apply to their Central Library in the same way as libraries in England and Wales apply to their regional bureau. Should the Scottish or the Irish Central Library be unable to lend a book the application is sent to the National Central Library, where the usual procedure is followed. The National Central Library has no direct contact with any library in Scotland or Ireland, other than an outlier or university library, and the Scottish and Irish Central Libraries do not normally make direct application to the outlier libraries.

CHAPTER VI

THE REGIONAL LIBRARY SYSTEMS[1]

THE introduction of the regional library systems may be classed among the five epoch-making events in the history of library development in the British Isles. The other four are the Public Libraries Act of 1850, the abolition of the rate limit in 1919, the institution of the County Library service in 1915, and the establishment of the Central Library for Students—now the National Central Library—in 1916.

As early as June 1926 the library authorities in Wales discussed at their Second Annual Conference the question of establishing a system of co-operation covering the whole of Wales and Monmouthshire, under which books would be lent between one library and another. Sir John Ballinger said that "any efficient system of co-operation would involve at some centre a catalogue of all the books in the libraries in a particular area. Assuming that Cardiff was made the regional library for Glamorgan and Monmouthshire, there ought to be in the public library at Cardiff a complete catalogue of all books in all the libraries in Glamorgan and Monmouthshire. When the librarian at Cardiff received a request from Neath for a book of a specific kind, he would refer to the union catalogue and find

[1] For a map of the regional systems see the frontispiece.

that the book was, perhaps, in Bedwellty. He would communicate with the librarian at Bedwellty and obtain the book, and so bring about active co-operation by means of union catalogues." Three committees were appointed (one for North, one for South, and one for West Wales) to consider the introduction of a regional library system for Wales. At the following conference all three committees presented favourable reports. Although this was the first step taken in the British Isles towards the establishment of a regional system, such a system was not actually founded in Wales until 1931.

In their Report,[1] issued in 1927, the Public Libraries Committee stated (Sections 440–442 and 445):

"We shall not be satisfied, however, by a mere extension of the practice (greatly though it is needed) of co-operation between adjoining libraries. That is only the foundation. We desire to see the library service go forward, by the linking up of these co-operating libraries into larger groups, each centred on some great library which may be conveniently described as a regional library; while all these groups or regions would again look to a common centre in the Central Library, which will be described in the following section.

"In a given area, such as a county, it will plainly be to the advantage of the weaker libraries if they are enabled to draw upon the resources of a stronger one. Duplication of the more expensive books and periodicals, and of those which are not in frequent demand, will be avoided, and

---

[1] Bibliography, No. 70.

REGIONAL LIBRARY SYSTEMS 85

the copies of such works in the larger libraries will be utilized more fully than if they are confined to the areas immediately served by those libraries. The basis of such a federation would naturally be a payment made by the weaker libraries to the stronger. In this way the stronger libraries will gain increased funds, while the weaker ones will gain an improved service of books.

"The regional library (if this term be accepted) in such a scheme will be the strongest library in the area concerned; and this, in the large majority of cases, will be the library of the principal borough.

"To avoid misconstruction, we would repeat that we do not recommend the compulsory imposition of a regional organization. We do, however, cordially recommend it for voluntary adoption. We are satisfied that all parties concerned in it stand to gain by such federation; and we believe that it is only by such co-operation that the national library service can attain the fullest development."

As will be seen later in this chapter, the lines on which the regional library systems have been established are not exactly those suggested by the Committee, but the general principle is much the same, and the Report undoubtedly expedited the system of co-operation which now links nearly all libraries into a great national system.

The earliest publication of importance on the regional systems is the Report on *Regional Libraries in England*,[1] issued by the Committee of the County Libraries Section of the Library Association in 1928. This Report created much interest at the time of its

[1] Bibliography, No. 71.

publication, and, although its recommendations were not all adopted in the form suggested, they were, undoubtedly, of material assistance to those taking an active part in the establishment of the early regional systems.

The Committee suggested that the time would soon come when the increasing calls made upon the National Central Library would be too great for one institution to deal with, and that a single channel of supply must ultimately lead to congestion and delay.

"We suggest," they said, "that the solution is in regional grouping. If the large libraries could be recruited as intermediary libraries, rather than outliers, they would relieve the Central Library by placing their stock of books at the disposal of the neighbouring libraries, and would in turn benefit by a better service from the Central Library, who would then be able to spend more of their funds on expensive books. The problem of locating copies of books could be overcome by joint cataloguing on a regional basis, and possible congestion would be relieved because the resources of the Central Library and its specialist outliers would only be called upon when local resources had been fully exploited.

"We would suggest," the Committee went on to say, "that the economic relations of large towns and surrounding districts are, with the development of modern transport, becoming more interdependent, and a considerable amount of money is being expended in the large towns by the surrounding populations. Thus the parochial point of view, although still present, is not so strong as heretofore, and we do not anticipate that there will be insuperable difficulties in arriving at some equitable arrangement.

"The libraries of the country would be organized on the following progressions: (1) local libraries co-operating within a given area, either by county or part of county; (2) large local library serving as regional library to one or more library groups; (3) large city libraries possibly serving as intermediaries or divisional libraries; (4) Central Library; (5) specialist outlier libraries.

"A joint catalogue would be required of the books in the libraries of the first stage, and would be kept at the regional library, or should such not exist, at the interchange library. An application for a book not in the stock at a local library would be forwarded to the regional or interchange library. They would locate the book and, if possible, arrange for its supply from the stock of the group libraries, before sending it from their own stock. If not available in either, the application would be forwarded to the Central Library to be dealt with."

The history of the regional library systems may be outlined quite briefly. As has already been mentioned, suggestions were made for the establishment of a regional system in Wales in 1926, but the first system to begin work was that of Cornwall in 1928. This system was so small (it now forms part of the South-Western Regional System) that it might almost be ignored were it not for the fact that it was the pioneer system. As such its success had considerable influence on those who took a leading part in the establishment of the first fully organized regional system in the four northern counties in January 1931.

The establishment of the Northern System is of some interest, because when its establishment was first considered it was not realized how full a scheme of co-operation would be established in the four northern counties, and how rapidly library authorities in other counties would follow the lead of the northern libraries. The following extract from the Sixteenth Annual Report of the Carnegie United Kingdom Trust, for the year 1929, shows how the Northern System originated.

"One other grant of a special kind deserves mention, namely, a grant of £1,000 to the Library of the Newcastle Literary and Philosophical Society. This is not a 'special' library in the ordinary sense, and, being owned by a body of members, appeared to be outside the scope of current policy. The Trustees, however, made a suggestion, which the Society readily accepted, namely, that if a grant were made, the Library should agree to act as a kind of Regional Central Library for the three counties of Cumberland, Durham, and Northumberland. The Trustees shortly afterwards called a Conference of all the Library Authorities and the leading Special Libraries of the area, with the objects of enabling the regional loan service to be fully discussed, and of ventilating the idea of a systematic scheme of co-operation throughout the three counties. The Conference produced an interesting discussion, and it was decided to examine the problem in detail at a subsequent conference. It may be added that the Society, having agreed to join in the above regional scheme, has voluntarily intimated willingness to lend through the Central Library for Students on the ordinary Outlier basis."

Other systems soon followed, with a result that by the end of the year 1936 the whole of England and

Wales was covered by a series of eight regional systems in addition to the London inter-lending system.[1] The following table gives the dates on which the systems began work:

1. NORTHERN. 1st January, 1931.
    Area covered: the 4 counties of Cumberland, Durham, Northumberland, Westmorland.
    Bureau housed at the Literary and Philosophical Society, Newcastle-upon-Tyne.
2. WEST MIDLAND. 1st April, 1931.
    Area covered: the 5 counties of Hereford, Shropshire, Stafford, Warwick, Worcester.
    Bureau housed at the Birmingham Public Library.
3. WALES. 1st January, 1932.
    Area covered: the 13 counties in Wales and Monmouthshire.
    National Bureau housed at the National Library of Wales, Aberystwyth.
    Sub-Bureau for South Wales housed at the Cardiff Public Library.
4. SOUTH-EASTERN. 1st October, 1933.
    Area covered: the 9 counties of Bedford, Berkshire, Buckingham, Essex, Hertford, Kent, Middlesex, Surrey, Sussex.
    Bureau housed at the National Central Library.
5. EAST MIDLAND. 1st January, 1935.
    Area covered: the 10 counties of Cambridge, Derby, Huntingdon, Leicester, Lincoln, Norfolk, Northampton, Nottingham, Rutland, Suffolk.
    Bureau housed at the Leicester Public Library.

[1] For a map of the regional systems see the frontispiece

6. YORKSHIRE. 1st April, 1935.
    Area covered: the whole of Yorkshire.
    Zonal centres at the Bradford, Hull, Leeds, and Sheffield Public Libraries.
7. NORTH-WESTERN. 1st April, 1935.
    Area covered: Lancashire, Cheshire, and the Isle of Man.
    Bureau housed at the Manchester Public Library.
8. SOUTH-WESTERN. Established in 1936 but work started on 1st April, 1937.
    Area covered: the 8 counties of Cornwall, Devon, Dorset, Gloucester, Hampshire (including the Isle of Wight), Oxford, Somerset, Wiltshire.
    Bureau housed at the Bristol Public Library.
9. LONDON INTER-LENDING SYSTEM. 1st November, 1934.
    Area covered: the 28 Metropolitan Boroughs and the Guildhall Library in the City of London.
    Bureau housed at the National Central Library.

The following table shows the number of libraries co-operating in the regional systems:

Regional System	Urban Libraries	County Libraries	University Libraries	Special Libraries	Total
Northern	21	3	3	7	34
West Midland	38	5	1	8	52
Wales	32	12	4	22	70
South-Eastern	58	10	—	—	68
East Midland	28	12	2	—	42
Yorkshire	35	3	3	—	41
North-Western	73	2	1	6	82
South-Western	29	8	2	—	39
London	26	—	—	—	26
	340	55	16	43	454

REGIONAL LIBRARY SYSTEMS

Only two county libraries, those of the Isle of Wight and the Isle of Man, are not yet co-operating in their regional system. Of the non-co-operating urban libraries, all except thirty-nine are in towns with a population of less than 20,000. Many of these libraries are so small that they could not offer any useful contribution to their regional systems, and some of them are libraries in name only.[1] The fifteen larger non-co-operating libraries are:

Bexley (pop. 65,000); Blackpool (pop. 130,000); Chesterfield (pop. 64,690); Greenwich (pop. 100,924); Grimsby (pop. 93,700); Ipswich (pop. 91,000); Lewisham (pop. 219,953); Newcastle-under-Lyme (pop. 53,000); Norwich (pop. 125,700); Shoreditch (pop. 97,042); Southend-on-Sea (pop. 140,000); West Ham (pop. 290,000); Willesden (pop. 195,295); Wimbledon (pop. 59,520); and Yarmouth (pop. 56,420).

Of these libraries, Ipswich, Norwich, and Southend-on-Sea are outlier libraries of the National Central Library. As such they are willing to lend books, but are not prepared to take full advantage of the great service offered by the regional systems.

The following table shows the total number of books lent during 1936 by libraries in regional areas to other libraries in the same area. The table does not include

---

[1] An account of some of these small libraries is given in L. Newcombe's "The Smaller urban libraries of England and Wales" on pages 507 to 510 of volume 2 (Fourth Series) of the *Library Association Record*, 1935.

books lent by or to libraries outside the particular regional area through the National Central Library:

Cornwall	1,504
East Midland	3,220
Northern	1,891
North-Western	4,421
South-Eastern	10,558
Wales	4,542
West Midland	4,215
Yorkshire	2,406
London	5,018
	37,775

Outside England and Wales progress has been less rapid. In Scotland the principle of a regional system for the whole country has been adopted by the library authorities, but it cannot be put into practice until Scottish library law (which differs from that of England and Wales) has been amended. A new Bill which has recently been drafted includes the following clause:

"Library authorities shall in addition to the powers already conferred upon them have the following powers:
(1) to participate in the establishment and activities and operation of (a) a Regional Library Bureau of Scotland for the promotion and attainment of co-operation between Scottish Libraries by arranging for the loan of books between participating Libraries, and (b) any National Central Lending Library for Scotland which may hereafter be established and to become members of such Bureau or National Library and

REGIONAL LIBRARY SYSTEMS

pay such subscriptions as may be required annually or otherwise. The powers conferred by this Sub-Section shall extend to and be exerciseable by the Scottish Universities' Libraries and by the Libraries of such Institutions as the Council of said Regional Library Bureau or National Library may approve."

No organized system of co-operation yet exists in Northern Ireland, although the establishment of a regional system was recommended by the Departmental Committee of the Government of Northern Ireland in their Report, issued in 1929.[1] The elements of such a system exist in the scheme drawn up in 1927, under which the Committee of the Belfast Public Library (who received a grant of £5,000 for the purpose from the Carnegie United Kingdom Trust) undertook to allow the library to act as a central library from which other libraries in Northern Ireland might draw non-fiction books on payment of threepence a volume. The scheme also proposed inter-lending of similar books between the urban and county libraries on payment of the cost of carriage by the borrowing library. So far very little use has been made of this service.

It may now be well to explain what a regional system is, and how it works.

In a regional library system the authorities of the libraries in a convenient geographical area agree to lend to one another, through their regional bureau, non-fiction books which are not easily accessible from any

[1] Bibliography, No. 28. See also p. 47.

other local source. The lending library reserves the full right to refuse the loan of any particular book. A study of the pamphlet dealing with the procedure for borrowing books (which is quoted in full in the Appendix) will show how simple the organization of the system is, and how the lending library is safeguarded against the loss or damage of books lent, and against the abuse of the privileges offered. Two important points must be borne in mind: (1) that a regional system is not intended to supply books which could, or should, be obtained locally; and (2) that no co-operating library should lend any book which its own readers are wanting.

Regional co-operation is not a device to save money for the National Central Library or any other library. Its sole object is to make it possible for each library to use its all-too-small book fund to the fullest possible advantage, whilst at the same time making use of books which may be lying idle in one library but urgently needed by a reader in another library.

The two things which are essential for the efficient working of a regional system are (1) a regional bureau, and (2) a union catalogue of all the non-fiction books in the co-operating libraries.

To a large extent the type, position, or size of the library in which the regional bureau is housed is of little importance. The ultimate object of regional co-operation is not to draw heavily upon the stock of one great library, but by means of a union catalogue to distribute the requests for loans among all the co-operating libraries. In the early stages, while the union catalogue is being built up, it is obviously an advantage to have the bureau in an exceptionally large library where one exists.

The main expense in establishing a regional system is that connected with the compilation of the nucleus union catalogue. Once that has been done, the annual expense of running the bureau is not great—though still a substantial sum—compared with the advantages gained. Fortunately the Carnegie Trustees have made generous grants towards the cost of building up the nucleus catalogues. Without these grants it is unlikely that any of the regional systems would have been established.

The problem of the size of a regional area is not so much a geographical one as one of library population and the ability of the libraries concerned to provide the necessary income for the upkeep of their bureau. As the service is almost entirely a postal one, the distance between one library and another is immaterial, except in the rare cases in which a telephone call is necessary.

The establishment of a regional library system presents certain difficulties, but experience has shown that these difficulties are not so serious as they at first appear, and that the advantages obtained give complete compensation. The most serious difficulty which was anticipated was that, whereas the large libraries

A SECTION OF THE NATIONAL UNION CATALOGUE, CONSISTING OF DUPLICATES OF ENTRIES IN THE REGIONAL UNION CATALOGUES, AT THE NATIONAL CENTRAL LIBRARY

would be called upon to lend many books, they would borrow very few in return. This, however, has not proved to be the case, as is shown by the following figures.

During the year 1936 the Newcastle Literary and Philosophical Society (at which the Northern Bureau is housed) borrowed no less than 255 books, and the Newcastle Public Library borrowed 125 books. It is true that during the same period these libraries lent 477 and 522 books respectively, but, apart from the time of the staff in sending off the books, these issues cost the libraries nothing, whereas the value of the books borrowed, at an average of fifteen shillings each (probably a low figure), comes to £191 5s. and £93 15s. respectively. These comparatively large figures, however, do not represent the true value of the service given, as many of the books are not on the market and could not be bought even at a very high price. Even such libraries as the Birmingham Public Library and the Manchester Public Library, which one might consider self-supporting with their great and valuable stock, borrowed 171 books and 142 books respectively.

The Yorkshire System is working for an experimental period of two years without a union catalogue. The quotations given below from the first Annual Report of the Yorkshire Regional Committee show that the system is providing a most satisfactory service. This, however, does not prove that those areas which make full use of their union catalogues are working on uneconomical or unsound lines. The success of the Yorkshire System is due solely to the generosity of the seven zonal libraries (that is, the Bradford, Hull, Leeds, and Sheffield Public Libraries; the libraries of the Universities of Leeds and Sheffield; and the library of University College, Hull), which undertake to lend all the books. So long as these libraries are prepared to provide the whole of the lending service there is no reason to suppose that the Yorkshire System cannot continue to function satisfactorily without a union catalogue. Such a system is, however, not a regional system of co-operation under which all libraries are able to take their full share in lending as well as borrowing. It also has the disadvantage of failing to provide any contribution to the national union catalogue, so that the National Central Library has no means of locating books in any of the Yorkshire libraries.

In their Report,[1] the Public Libraries Committee suggested, in 1927, that co-operation between the London Borough libraries might "take the form of free inter-loans of books, which can only become fully effective if a union catalogue of the London libraries can be brought into existence through the deposit in a central bureau of duplicate cards from each library."

At a meeting held on May 9, 1929, attended by representatives of the Metropolitan Boroughs and the

[1] Page 154 of Bibliography, No. 70.

Guildhall Library, it was resolved that a union catalogue of the non-fiction books in all the London libraries should be compiled and housed at the National Central Library. Work was begun in March 1930, and in November 1934 the financial responsibility for the upkeep of the catalogue was taken over by the Metropolitan Boroughs' Standing Joint Committee, and an inter-lending system was inaugurated. The difference between the London inter-lending system and a regional system is that, whereas libraries in the latter are willing to lend their books to a library in any other regional system, the London libraries—except those which are outlier libraries to the National Central Library—limit their loans to other libraries in London; a difference which is both important and unfortunate.

The method by which a reader obtains a book through his regional system is described in Chapter x, and the way in which the regional catalogues are built up is dealt with on page 133.

The work of the Regional Committees is co-ordinated by means of the National Committee on Regional Library Co-operation, the membership of which consists of the chairman and the secretary of each Regional Committee, and two representatives each of the London Inter-Lending System, the Joint Standing Committee on [University] Library Co-operation, the Library Association, the Carnegie United Kingdom Trust, and the National Central Library. The librarian of the National Central Library is a member of all the Regional Committees, and is thus able to assist in the co-ordination of their work and that of the National Central Library.

It may be thought that now that the regional systems are giving so excellent a service there is less need for the National Central Library, but the demand made upon the Library during the year 1936 by no means supports this assumption. We find that in spite of the 37,775 books issued through the regional bureaux, the National Central Library lent more books. This aggregate increase is, perhaps, a natural outcome of the greater demand which the establishment of the regional systems has by making more widely known the possibility of obtaining books once beyond the reach of so many readers.

Since the establishment of the regional systems the value of each book supplied by the National Central Library is altogether higher. "Value" does not necessarily refer to the price of the book, though that is a good deal higher on the average, but rather to its scarcity. It stands to reason that with the development of the regional systems and the growth of the union catalogues an increasingly large proportion of the more generally used books can be supplied from within the regions, with a result that the books for which the National Central Library is asked consist mainly of scarce and highly-specialized books. This does not mean that such books are not supplied from within the regions. They are; especially from the larger urban libraries, and the university and special libraries. But the number of such books obtainable locally is necessarily—and rightly—small. It is not the business of the local library to buy an expensive, specialized, or foreign book wanted by one reader but not likely to be used by any other local reader. That is the business of a central pool, from which such a book may well be wanted later on for readers in other parts of the British Isles.

Decentralization of the work was not essential, or even necessarily desirable, so far as the National Central Library itself was concerned. Given a sufficient income, a central organization could do most of the work now being done by the regional bureaux, so far as the lending of books is concerned. But the regional systems are doing something more than the mere lending of books and the compiling of union catalogues, important as these two functions are. They are doing something a central organization could never do, and something which means a great deal for the library movement of the country—they are bringing together authorities and librarians of libraries of all types and sizes on regional committees and at annual meetings, where they have learned to appreciate one another's problems and to help one another in many ways. The establishment of the regional systems has also done a great deal to arouse a wider interest in the library movement, which has thus been given a publicity it would not otherwise have had. So, quite apart from the question of lending books, the regional systems are well worth while.

The regional systems are part of a great national service, just as the National Central Library itself is. The two are inter-dependent, and the one cannot now function adequately without the other. The regional systems have been responsible for a most encouraging increase in the demand for a type of book all librarians are particularly glad to lend. That demand will, it is believed, continue to increase as the great national system of co-operation becomes better known. In 1936 the regional systems lent 37,775 books to libraries within their own region, apart from 5,502 books lent to libraries outside their region through the agency of the National Central Library. The newer systems are still far from being in full working order, and there can be no doubt that when they are the service given by the regional movement will be much greater than it is now.

In addition to the national service described in this chapter and the university libraries inter-lending system dealt with in Chapter VII, there are several smaller but still most useful systems of co-operation between groups of local or special libraries. Such systems are doing good work, and are in no way inconsistent with the larger regional systems with which many of them are co-operating. Co-operation between county and small neighbouring urban libraries, usually taking the form of borrowing a fixed number of books by the latter in return for an agreed annual payment to the county library, is fairly common; but this type of co-operation is outside the scope of this book.

The earliest of the smaller systems of any importance appears to be that established by the libraries of Mansfield, Newark, and Worksop early in 1927. Later Chesterfield joined the group. Under this system any non-fiction book, not wanted by a local reader, will be lent by one library to another at a charge of twopence a volume. A union catalogue of the non-fiction books, in sheaf form, has been compiled and a copy is kept in each library.

In 1928 the Wiltshire County Library and the Salisbury and Calne Public Libraries (the only public libraries in Wiltshire) entered into an arrangement for the inter-lending of non-fiction books. A union catalogue is housed at the County Library.

In January 1929 a system of co-operation was established between the libraries of Ipswich, King's Lynn, Lowestoft, Norwich, and Great Yarmouth, under which books may be lent from one library to another at a uniform charge per book. Any library buying an expensive book informs the other libraries in order to avoid unnecessary duplication within the area. The librarians meet from time to time to discuss matters of mutual interest.

A system of co-operation was adopted by Accrington,

THE REGIONAL LIBRARY SYSTEMS 103

Blackburn, and Burnley in March 1929. The system provides for the inter-lending of books (asked for by telephone, and sent by tram or carrier), and co-operation in buying expensive books and periodicals. Several other systems, such as the Thames Valley System, have been established within the past few years. Some of these are now merged in their regional system.

Systems of co-operation of a more specialized nature include that arranged between the libraries of five of the larger London Polytechnics in 1933. Under this scheme the National Central Library is not asked for a book which can be lent by one of the co-operating libraries. Another system is the one inaugurated in 1932 by the Sheffield Public Library[1] under which books may be borrowed from the Public Library, the University Library, and the libraries of several organizations and large firms in Sheffield; the object of the system being to assist the technical staff of the co-operating firms. A somewhat similar system has recently been introduced in Manchester,[2] under which books are lent between nine of the leading industrial firms. The value of this system is increased by direct co-operation with the National Central Library.

[1] Bibliography, Nos. 7 and 125.   [2] Ibid., No. 127.

CHAPTER VII

THE UNIVERSITY LIBRARIES INTER-LENDING SYSTEM

THE system of co-operation between the university libraries is one of considerable importance, and one in which almost every university and university institution in the British Isles is taking an active part. Its origin is outlined on page 59.

The university inter-lending system is organized on lines somewhat similar to those of the regional systems—the National Central Library taking the place of the regional bureau—except that the libraries concerned are a class and not a geographical group. The other main differences are the absence of a union catalogue—other than one for periodicals—and the method of obtaining a book, once it is located, by the National Central Library. Students' text-books, the more general reference books, and the current numbers of periodicals are outside the scope of the system, but any other book may be asked for, and usually obtained. The librarian sends an application form to the National Central Library, which, if unable to supply the book from its own shelves, or, in the case of a periodical, to trace it in the union catalogue of periodicals, includes the author, title, and such other details as are available and necessary, on the next "University List," the details of which are described on pages 63 to 66. Lists are regularly sent to thirty-five university libraries, two different lists going each week. In addition, select lists often go to the more specialized university libraries, such as the Courtauld Institute of Art, the Jews' College, the London School of Economics, the London School of Hygiene, the School of Oriental Studies, the School of Slavonic Studies, schools of agriculture, and schools of medicine, if the books wanted are likely to be found in such libraries.

On the return of the lists, the National Central Library does not arrange for the book to be sent from the library possessing a copy to the library needing it, but gives the librarian of the latter the name of the library willing to lend a copy. The reason for adopting this method, rather than the one under which the book would be sent direct to the library needing it, is that in the case of the university libraries the reader often does not want the book at once. He may be working on a long bibliography and his immediate need is to know, through his librarian, where he can obtain the books when he is ready for them. Often he collects this information during the term ready to start work in the vacation, when he will have more time for his research.

In addition to the inter-university system, the university libraries have access to the normal service of the National Central Library, that is, its own books and those of its outlier libraries. University libraries which are co-operating in a regional system, or which are outlier libraries, also have access to the regional bureaux. In return, they make a substantial contribution to the general system of library co-operation by lending books to public and other libraries through the regional bureaux or the National Central Library.

The "University Lists" are ruled in five columns, the first for a running number, the second for details of the book required, the third for the name of the library wanting the book, the fourth for the librarian to whom the enquiry is sent to put "Yes" if he has the book but is unable to lend it, and the fifth for him to put "Yes" if he is able to lend it. Each list contains an average of forty entries.

CHAPTER VIII

INTERNATIONAL LIBRARY LOANS

THIS branch of the work of the National Central Library is one of great importance, although, at present, the figures are small. The subject is dealt with only briefly here, as anyone desiring more detailed information should refer to Mr. Pafford's book on library co-operation in Europe,[1] particularly Chapter II. This book gives full information, historical and practical, about the international system in which almost every European country, the United States of America, and other countries are taking a more or less active part. Our concern with the subject is that side which affects the libraries of the British Isles. Readers will, however, find it well worth while to read Mr. Pafford's book, from which they will obtain a broader view of a most important side of modern library work.

Although, so far as the British Isles are concerned, there is a steady increase, the figures of international loans are, rightly, small. The reason for this is that the international service is put into operation only after it has been ascertained that no copy of the book is available for loan in the country from which the enquiry originates. In order that the comparatively

[1] Bibliography, No. 85.

costly international machinery may not be abused, no application is, normally, dealt with unless it comes through the applicant's national centre. This procedure acts as a guarantee that a book is not being sent to a library in a country already possessing a loanable copy or copies. It also avoids unnecessary correspondence between individual librarians, and, in most cases, it is both quicker and cheaper to use the recognized centres which possess the means—in most cases still far from perfect, but yet most useful—of locating books.

The National Central Library never applies for a book from abroad unless specially requested to do so by the borrowing librarian; first because the reader or his library may not be prepared to pay the additional cost of postage and possibly insurance, and secondly because he may not be able to wait for the book to come. This, combined with the fact that the national service in Great Britain is becoming more efficient each year, means that the number of books needed by British libraries from libraries abroad is never likely to be large.

When asked to try to obtain a book from abroad, the National Central Library communicates, not with a library known or believed to contain a copy, but with the appropriate national centre. For instance, if the book wanted is a German one it is assumed—unless information is available to suggest otherwise—that a copy will most readily be obtained from a library in Germany. Application is, therefore, made to the Auskunftsbureau [Enquiry Office] at the State Library in Berlin. This office will, probably, be able to locate a copy by means of its great union catalogue of books in the libraries of Germany. If it is successful, it will give the name of the library concerned to the National Central Library, which will then get into direct touch with a view to arranging the loan of the book. In the same way, a library in Germany will approach the National Central Library through the Auskunftsbureau for the loan of a book from a library in Great Britain. One actual case will illustrate the value of this international co-operation. The Kendal Public Library has recently on three occasions been able to lend books to the University of Heidelberg. A few years ago the possibility of a small library such as that of Kendal (with about 20,000 non-fiction books) being able to help a great university library containing over 1,000,000 volumes would have been remote.

The following table shows the number of books lent between British and foreign libraries, and the countries participating, from 1931, when the National Central Library became the recognized centre for international loans, to 1936.

	Books lent by British libraries to	Books borrowed by British libraries from
Algeria	1	—
Austria	35	12
Belgium	209	10
Bulgaria	1	—
Chile	—	1
Czechoslovakia	18	5
Denmark	168	11
Finland	—	3
France	56	43
Germany	202	274
Holland	240	22
Hungary	—	3
India	3	—
Italy	18	18
Japan	—	1
Kenya	4	—
Norway	3	2
Palestine	1	2
Poland	61	9
Roumania	—	1
Russia	31	14
Spain	—	1
Sweden	16	2
Switzerland	47	21
Transvaal	21	1
United States of America	6	22
Yugoslavia	—	1
Twenty-seven countries	1,141	479

INTERNATIONAL LIBRARY LOANS

An analysis of the 1,141 books lent by British libraries shows that they were obtained from the following sources:

The National Central Library's own stock	201
Outlier Libraries	380
University Libraries	560
	1,141

CHAPTER IX

UNION CATALOGUES

As there are still some persons who doubt the wisdom of attempting to compile union catalogues, it may be well to open this chapter with a few notes on the relative value of such catalogues and the cost of their production. Actually few, if any, persons doubt their value as a means of obtaining books quickly: the doubtful point is, rather, whether the money and time devoted to their compilation is justified. It must be admitted that they *are* expensive, not so much in regard to the cost of the material—cards and cabinets, or paper slips and binders—which, after all, is not a big item, but more especially on account of the salaries of the headquarters staff and—a point liable to be overlooked when calculating the cost of compilation—the value of the time of the staff of all the libraries concerned in supplying entries for their books.

Fortunately union cataloguing in Great Britain has reached a stage at which it is possible to give actual facts instead of having to express opinions and discuss a theory. These facts would seem to indicate that not only is the cost of compilation fully justified, but that efficient and economical co-operation is impossible without union catalogues. This opinion was held in the United States, Germany, and elsewhere many years before any attempt was made to compile a union catalogue on a large scale in this country. It may be suggested that the Yorkshire zonal system (for details of which see pages 96 to 97) works well and cheaply without a union catalogue. The answer is that the Yorkshire system is not a system of full co-operation, but one under which many libraries depend upon the generosity of a few large ones and have no opportunity to contribute their share to the common pool—much, it may be added, to their regret. This system, making no contribution to the national union catalogue, is thus unable to take its full share in the national system. No criticism is made of the Yorkshire system, which is an experiment of great importance and interest, and one well worth making. But if it proves successful, that success will be no argument against the value of union catalogues, because in no other regional area is a group of large libraries prepared to shoulder the whole burden of lending, even if that were desirable.

It has been argued that union catalogues are not worth while because: (a) The smaller libraries will not have any books which are not in the larger ones and the larger ones will all have the same books, and (b) as a consequence of (a) the large libraries will have to do all the lending and will receive nothing in return. Let us see how this works out in practice in the regional systems which are making full use of their union catalogues. We will deal with (a) first.

The Report of the Northern Regional Library Committee for 1935 stated that

"Of a total of 109,600 entries dealt with by the union catalogue staff during the year, 54,395 were duplicates of entries already in the catalogue and 55,205 represented new entries. After five years of compilation, it is a matter of special interest that the percentage of new entries continues to be so high. The catalogue of South Shields Public Library, now in process of incorporation, is producing 40 per cent new entries, even though the catalogues of such public libraries as Newcastle, Sunderland, Gateshead and Middlesbrough have already been incorporated. The catalogue of the Literary and Philosophical Society is producing 55 per cent new entries, while 90 per cent of the Durham University Routh Collection is entirely new. The percentage of new entries in the lists of additions to stock sent to the Bureau varies from 30 per cent to 80 per cent according to the nature of the library."

A recent examination of the catalogue, covering thirty-two libraries, indicates that

70 per cent		1 copy only
17 per cent	of the books are represented by	2 copies only
3 per cent		3 copies only
10 per cent		4 or more copies

An examination was recently made of the catalogue at the National Bureau of the Welsh Regional System. The entries for 4,000 books in letters A and B, covering eighteen libraries, were analysed, with the following result:

84·425 per cent	(3,377)		1 copy only
10·8 per cent	(432)		2 copies only
2·75 per cent	(110)	of the books are represented by	3 copies only
0·975 per cent	(39)		4 copies only
0·625 per cent	(25)		5 copies only
0·175 per cent	(7)		6 copies only
0·125 per cent	(5)		7 copies only
0·075 per cent	(3)		8 copies only
0·025 per cent	(1)		9 copies only
0·025 per cent	(1)		10 or more copies

The editor of the Glamorgan and Monmouthshire section of the Welsh union catalogue (which includes most of the large libraries in Wales) stated in his report for 1935 that on completion of the first letter (A) the following analysis of the number of copies of the same book contained in the various libraries was made:

66·6 per cent		1 copy only
19·7 per cent		2 copies only
7·4 per cent		3 copies only
2·8 per cent	of the books are represented by	4 copies only
1·4 per cent		5 copies only
0·9 per cent		6 copies only
0·7 per cent		7 copies only
0·2 per cent		8 copies only
0·2 per cent		9 copies only
0·1 per cent		10 or more copies

The number of libraries covered by this table is twenty-four, and the number of entries analysed approximately 4,000. No single book is shown as being in every library, the largest number of libraries for a single book being seventeen. Cases have come to light where copies of more or less well-known books are to be found in the smaller libraries only.

The experience of the South Eastern Regional Bureau is much the same, though perhaps even more striking, as the number of libraries included in the union catalogue at the date of the report was fifty-one, a large proportion of which are libraries of much the same size and type.

"It is believed," the Regional Committee stated in their Report for 1934–35, "that the opinion is still held in some quarters that duplication of stock among the participant libraries is so great as to make a union catalogue unnecessary and wasteful. Your Committee believe that this argument is fundamentally unsound and, in order to produce convincing proof of this, have had statistics compiled of the duplication in letter A of the catalogue.

40·22 per cent		1 copy only
14·3 per cent		2 copies only
9·21 per cent		3 copies only
6·33 per cent		4 copies only
4·6 per cent		5 copies only
3·43 per cent	of the books	6 copies only
2·8 per cent	are	7 copies only
2·42 per cent	represented	8 copies only
2·29 per cent	by	9 copies only
1·65 per cent		10 copies only
9·82 per cent		11–20 copies only
2·34 per cent		21–30 copies only
0·53 per cent		31–40 copies only
0·06 per cent		40 or more copies

In the East Midland Regional System an analysis of the entries for 4,000 books in the letter A reveals the fact that 53·95 per cent of the books are represented by one copy only. The number of libraries covered, however, is less than that of the South Eastern, as the entries analysed represent the complete stocks of twenty-nine libraries and the partial stocks of eight others. The following is a detailed result of the analysis:

53·95 per cent	(2,158)		1 copy only
14·75 per cent	(590)		2 copies only
9·075 per cent	(363)		3 copies only
5·5 per cent	(220)		4 copies only
3·9 per cent	(156)		5 copies only
2·35 per cent	(94)		6 copies only
2·5 per cent	(100)	of the books	7 copies only
1·275 per cent	(51)	are	8 copies only
1·25 per cent	(50)	represented	9 copies only
1·125 per cent	(45)	by	10 copies only
0·95 per cent	(38)		11 copies only
0·675 per cent	(27)		12 copies only
0·6 per cent	(24)		13 copies only
0·3 per cent	(12)		14 copies only
0·4 per cent	(16)		15 copies only
0·325 per cent	(13)		16 copies only

The remaining 1·075 per cent of the books are represented in from seventeen to twenty-nine libraries.

Another table, compiled from the London Public Libraries Union Catalogue, also shows the comparatively small percentage of duplication among a particular group of libraries. This is all the more surprising as the libraries concerned are of much the same type —though they vary in size—and cater for the public of the Metropolis. The entries checked—which represent a section of the completed catalogue for the thirty libraries— were taken from the letter A.

50·8 per cent		1 copy only
13·2 per cent		2 copies only
7·4 per cent		3 copies only
4·8 per cent	of the books	4 copies only
3·8 per cent	are	5 copies only
3·2 per cent	represented	6 copies only
2·5 per cent	by	7 copies only
2·1 per cent		8 copies each
1·8 per cent		9 copies only
10·4 per cent		10 or more copies

Only 0·05 per cent of the books are in all the thirty libraries. From an analysis of a representative section of the catalogue it is computed that over 112,000 books are represented by one copy only; that nearly 30,000 are represented by two copies only; and that over 16,000 are represented by three copies only. Books of which copies are in more than half of the Metropolitan public libraries number less than 10,000.

The following table shows the percentage of books represented by a single copy in the regional union catalogues:

Region	Number of libraries	Percentage of single copies
Wales (National)	18	84·425
Northern	32	70
Wales (Cardiff)	24	66·6
East Midland	29	53·95
London	30	50·8
South-Eastern	51	40·22

Now let us look at suggestion (*b*): that the larger libraries will do all the lending and will receive nothing in return.

In the first year (1931) of the Northern system all the books obtained within the region came from nine libraries, and only four of these lent more than seven books each. 66·16 per cent (614 out of 928) came from the library of the Literary and Philosophical Society at which the bureau is situated. In the second year the number of lending libraries had increased to fifteen; in the third year to twenty; in the fourth to twenty-four; and in the fifth (1935) to thirty-two, of which eight lent over 100 books each. Although in the fifth year the number of books lent had increased to 2,362 (two and a half times as many as in the first year), the Literary and Philosophical Society's contribution had dropped to 375 (15·87 per cent). All the borrowing libraries, except two very small ones in towns with a population of 3,239 and 6,581 respectively, had lent books. This marked and steady increase coincides with the growth of the union catalogue, and, of course, the proper use being made of the catalogue by the bureau staff. It is particularly interesting to note that the libraries which have not lent are those whose books are not yet included in the union catalogue.

In 1935, twenty-one of the thirty-two borrowing libraries in the Glamorgan and Monmouthshire section of the Welsh Regional System also lent books. In the first year (1932)—when the union catalogue was in its infancy—the Cardiff Public Library, at which the bureau is housed, lent no less than 89·4 per cent of the books. By 1935 the Cardiff percentage had dropped to 63·6, and with the growth of the union catalogue it is likely that this percentage will continue to drop.

The South Eastern figures for 1936 show that every one of the sixty-seven co-operating libraries has lent books. As the union catalogue grows, the number of books obtained from the smaller libraries increases. It is noteworthy also that the percentage of books supplied from within the region increases as the catalogue grows. In the first quarter (April–June 1934) the system lent 36·3 per cent of the books asked for, but, solely as a result of the growth of the union catalogue, this percentage had increased to 73 during the quarter October to December 1936. During this period the number of entries in the catalogue had grown from 43,000 to 115,000.

In the first year (1935) twenty-five of the forty borrowing libraries in the East Midland System lent books, in spite of the fact that work on the union catalogue was only begun during the year. Although, until the catalogue has made more headway, the Leicester Public Library, at which the bureau is housed, will necessarily be the largest individual lender, 55·7 per cent of the books lent have come from other libraries in the system. Once the union catalogue is completed there is no reason to suppose that any one library will lend more than its reasonable share of books.

In London all the libraries (with the exception of the Guildhall Library, which does not lend books) take an active part in lending.

Union catalogues are well worth the expense in material and labour involved in their compilation, and are essential if inter-library lending is to be developed on sound lines with every library taking its share in lending as well as borrowing, and with the possibility of books being traced quickly and economically. None of the alternatives provides a satisfactory substitute. These alternatives are:

(*a*) The circulation at regular intervals of lists of books wanted. Lists are already in use by the National Central Library and some of the regional systems, but only as a temporary measure pending the completion of the union catalogue. Such lists are, however, far from satisfactory, first because they are a slow method of obtaining the required information, and, secondly, because they waste the time of librarians all over the country who have to check the same lists to see whether they have any of the books. The aggregate time spent in checking a single list of, say, fifty entries in 100 different libraries, allowing half a minute (probably too short a time) for each title would be forty-one hours and forty minutes. With the use of lists, time—sometimes running into many days—must elapse before replies are received from *all* libraries, but in the case of most applications time may not be a factor of great importance. A further difficulty, already experienced by the South Eastern Bureau, is that books reported as being available may have been issued by the libraries before an application for their loan is received from the bureau. If, in order to avoid this difficulty, librarians guarantee to reserve all books they report, they may be withholding books from their own readers which will not, after all, be required for regional loan. It may be questioned whether the method of circulating lists is less costly than finding books by a union catalogue. The cost of the list method includes (*a*) postage, duplicating materials, and stationery, (*b*) the time taken in compiling and typing the lists, (*c*) the time spent by the staff in many libraries in checking, marking, and returning the lists, (*d*) the time spent by the bureau staff dealing with lists when returned. In addition, many days must be wasted in arranging for the loan of a book traced by means of a list as compared with the loan of a book found in a union catalogue, which can usually be sent off the following day.

(*b*) Postcards, either one to each library or one to circulate. The former is an expensive method which is also unsatisfactory for the same reasons as the lists, and the latter is, among other shortcomings, very slow.

(c) The telephone. On the ground of expense this is out of the question for other than local calls, and even for local calls the number of libraries to which enquiries could be made would be few. Imagine the time spent by an assistant at the National Central Library or a regional bureau and an assistant at a library trying to check on the telephone a list of thirty, forty, or perhaps more books, some in foreign languages. Imagine also the confusion and mistakes that would arise from one end of the list to the other!

(d) Depending upon one large library (as in the case of the West Midland Regional System) or a small group of large libraries (as in the case of the Yorkshire Regional System) for all, or nearly all, the books. It is, of course, not co-operation at all if one library lends all the books, and it is co-operation only in a limited sense where the lending is restricted to a few libraries.

Union catalogues may be expensive to compile—but not excessively so—but most of the alternatives are also expensive and none of them is satisfactory. Moreover, union catalogues have a bibliographical value which has not yet been fully utilized. One way in which the catalogues when completed may be of service is as a means of avoiding the unnecessary duplication of expensive books. Although the compilation of a catalogue entails a great deal of work in the initial stages it is, once it is compiled, the means of saving a great deal of time to the staff of the bureau, thus reducing the cost of maintenance. It is also the means of supplying the material for building up the national union catalogue at the National Central Library. Much instructive information on the value of union catalogues will be found on pages 102 to 116 of Mr. Pafford's book.[1]

In 1935, Mr. W. Hynes, in a paper read before the London and Home Counties Branch of the Library Association,[2] said:

"One can conceive a multitude of uses for the regional catalogue apart from its primary use at regional headquarters. It provides an up-to-date list of duplicates within an area, useful when considering withdrawals from stock. It provides a list of little-wanted books which only the specialist or very large library need keep. It gives particulars of all the editions of any one book possessed by the libraries within the area. On the other hand it shows gaps in stock and might be helpful in ensuring that they be filled, and would help also to prevent the discarding of a rare book."

We will now see something of the way in which the various union catalogues are being compiled. First we might consider a few general points which apply to all the British catalogues. The word catalogue is not altogether a satisfactory one; "finding list" would

[1] Bibliography, No. 91.   [2] Ibid., No. 33.

better describe these great sources of information, their chief function being, not to give detailed bibliographical information, but to enable the staffs of the National Central Library and the Regional Bureaux to find out where books are. With the exception of one or two of the printed catalogues, all the union catalogues, or finding lists, contain author entries only; no attempt being made to provide anything in the nature of subject indexes. Such a task would be tremendous and to be done efficiently would necessitate access to the books themselves and not merely to catalogue entries. The entries are for non-fiction books only, an endeavour being made in each catalogue to include an entry for each such book in the libraries covered by the catalogue. The information given in most of the catalogues is limited to such essential information as (1) the full name of the author; (2) brief title of the book; (3) number of the edition if not the first; (4) place of publication; and (5) date. Some of the catalogues also include the name of the editor or translator, if any.

The entries are in one of three forms: (1) 5-inch by 3-inch cards housed in card cabinets; (2) 8-inch by 4-inch paper slips contained in binders; or (3) printed books or cyclostyled lists, which are for the most part restricted to small or specialized catalogues.

The only national union catalogues on cards are the London Public Libraries Union Catalogue, the Catalogue of the Outlier Libraries (both housed at the National Central Library), and the Welsh Regional Catalogue. The London Union Catalogue was the first of the great union catalogues in this country. Work was begun in March 1930, with a staff of one chief cataloguer and two assistants. Many of the thirty libraries (that is, the twenty-eight Metropolitan Borough Libraries, the Guildhall Library, and the Minet Library, which is a joint library between Lambeth and Camberwell) provided the necessary entries on 5-inch by 3-inch slips issued by the Catalogue Committee. Some libraries, however, were unable to spare members of the staff to do this work. In such cases a member of the catalogue staff visited the library and copied the entries from the catalogue, or the information was obtained from printed catalogues supplied for the use of the catalogue staff.

At the end of four and a half years, that is, by October 1934, the nucleus catalogue was nearing completion. Up to this date the whole of the cost had been met by a grant from the Carnegie United Kingdom Trust. The Committee were faced with the problem of the upkeep of the catalogue. This was solved by the control and financial responsibility for the catalogue being taken over, in November 1934, by the Metropolitan Boroughs' Standing Joint Committee. This event marks the first occasion on which the Metropolitan Borough Councils agreed to any form of co-operation in library matters. Under the

UNION CATALOGUES

scheme of co-operation instituted by the Metropolitan Boroughs' Standing Joint Committee all except three of the London Borough Libraries now lend books to one another through the agency of the bureau established in connection with the union catalogue.

A word about the cost of building up this great catalogue may be useful. The cards are thick and of the best quality. It would be a mistake to use a poor quality card when, probably, 90 per cent of the cost of any union catalogue is represented by labour and not material. Six hundred thousand specially printed cards cost £413. As in the case of the cards, it is, in the long run, an economy to obtain the best material and workmanship for the cabinets to house the cards. The cabinets for all the cards at the National Central Library have been specially designed to give the maximum capacity on the minimum floor space. This object is achieved by making the cabinets thirteen drawers high, the bottom of the lowest drawer being 1 foot $2\frac{1}{2}$ inches from the floor, and the top of the highest drawer 5 feet 5 inches from the floor. This makes the top drawer too high to be consulted comfortably by a person of average height. To overcome this difficulty a step runs the full length of each section of cabinets, a section being 40 feet 6 inches long, containing 1,001 drawers, capable of holding 1,001,000 cards. This step, covered with linoleum, is 12 inches deep and just below the bottom drawer. By standing on the step the top drawers can easily be consulted and it does not interfere with the use of the lower drawers. It must be remembered that these catalogues are for staff use only: the step method would not be recommended for public use. An illustration of a section of this catalogue will be found facing page 80.

On the lower half of the cards used for the London Union Catalogue are a number of abbreviations representing the thirty co-operating libraries. The libraries possessing a copy of the book catalogued are indicated by underlining in ink the appropriate abbreviation. For instance, the card shown opposite indicates that the book is in the Chelsea, Hackney, and Westminster Libraries. If at a later date a copy is added to any other library, the appropriate abbreviation is underlined. The stroke through GUIL shows that there is no longer a copy in the Guildhall Library, which once had the book.

This simple and labour-saving method of showing where books are works admirably, but it could not be adopted on a 5-inch by 3-inch card for more than about thirty libraries.

There are at present 1,328,000 entries in the London Union Catalogue, but this figure includes a great many duplicates for the same book. These will eventually be copied from the slips on to the permanent cards.

Now let us see what the compilation of this catalogue on cards has cost. The following figures show the expenditure up to the time when the catalogue was

PAFFORD, John Henry Pyle.
Library co-operation in Europe.
1935.

BATT	DEPT	HACK		KENS	PADD	STEP
BERM	FINS	HAMM		LAMB	PANC	STOK
BETH	FULH	HAMP		LEWI	POPL	WAND
CAMB	GREE	HOLB		MARY	SHOR	WEST
CHEL	~~GUY~~	ISLI	○	MINE	SOUT	WOOL

A card in the London Public Libraries Union Catalogue. The card is reproduced full size, that is 5 ins. by 3 ins.

practically complete and was taken over by the Metropolitan Boroughs' Standing Joint Committee.

	£ s. d.	£ s. d.
Salaries for four years and seven months	.. ..	2,750 0 0
546-drawer card cabinet, each drawer holding 1,000 cards	405 10 0	
600,000 5-in. by 3-in. cards ..	413 0 0	
1,590,000 5-in. by 3-in. paper slips	98 14 0	
3,000 guide cards	43 10 0	
Sundry equipment	40 17 8	
		1,001 11 8
Postages, travelling and sundries		124 13 8
		£3,876 5 4

Little need be said about the union catalogue of the outlier libraries, which is housed in cabinets similar to those used for the London Union Catalogue. The cards are feint-ruled, but contain no printed matter, the location of the book being shown by appropriate letters at the top right-hand corner. For instance, L.S. shows that the book is in the Linnean Society, S.A. in the Society of Antiquaries, and so on. In addition to entries for books in the outlier libraries, this catalogue also contains an entry—made by the staff of the National Central Library—for each book located by the Library for which there is not already an entry in one of the union catalogues. These entries are most useful if the same book is asked for again. The other entries in this catalogue are supplied by some of the outlier libraries, and consist largely of copies of accession cards. So far, the staff of the National Central Library have been able to do little to build up this catalogue, which, as a result, contains only about 160,000 entries for the 6,500,000 volumes in the outlier libraries.

We will now turn to the second form of union catalogues, that is, the sheaf catalogue, consisting of entries on 8-inch by 4-inch paper sheets housed in binders. Probably the large majority of persons who have had any considerable experience in the use of catalogues, other than printed catalogues, will agree that a card catalogue is much better than a sheaf catalogue. It is easier to insert and withdraw entries, and the durability of the cards and the cabinets is altogether greater than that of paper sheets and binders. But in a great union catalogue which will, eventually, contain several million entries, the sheaf form has three important advantages.

The first of these is the cost of the material. A thoroughly good binder, bought in large quantities, can be obtained for two shillings. Each binder will contain 430 sheets. The sheets, printed as shown on page 132, cost about 4s. 6d. a thousand. The second advantage is the economy of floor space occupied by the catalogue, and the third, and by far the most important, is the ease with which a number of copies of the catalogue can be obtained at a small additional expenditure of time and money. The value of this will be realized from the following outline of the way in which the

RYE, Reginald Arthur

The students' guide to the libraries of London.
3rd ed. 1927.

RYE,
R.A.

1	2	3	4	5	6	7	8	9	10	11	12	13	14	15	16	17	18	19	20
21	22	23	24	25	26✻	27	28	29	30	31 /1910	32	33	34	35	36✻	37	38	39	40✻
41✻	42✻	43	44	45	46	47	48 /1908	49	50	51	52✻	53	54	55	56	57	58	59	60
61	62	63	64	65	66	67✻	68	69	70	71	72	73	74 /1910	75	76	77	78	79	80
81	82	83	84	85	86	87	88	89	90	91	92	93	94	95	96	97	98	99	100

An entry in a regional union catalogue. The libraries containing the book are indicated by a star in the appropriate numbered square. If a library possesses a copy of an edition of the book other than the one mentioned in the entry, the date is put in the numbered square instead of a star. The size of the original sheet is 8 inches by 4 inches.

UNION CATALOGUES

regional catalogues (with the exception of the one in Wales, which is on cards) are being compiled.

At each regional bureau (except the Yorkshire one) a union catalogue of all the non-fiction books is being compiled. In most of the bureaux four copies of each entry are made, one original copy and three carbons. The original copy is kept at the bureau and forms the regional union catalogue. The first carbon copy, which is on a different colour sheet in each region, is sent to the National Central Library where the sheets are sorted into one alphabetical order. Already this national union catalogue contains over 500,000 entries. In a year or two the total is likely to run into two or three million. The other two carbon copies are circulated, in two groups, among the libraries in the regional area. On receipt of a batch of entries a library checks them with its own catalogue and puts a cross in the square containing the number representing the library. The sheets are then sent on to the next library in the circuit and eventually work their way back to the regional bureau, where the information is copied on to the bureau copy of the catalogue. Books in any library which are not already represented in the circulated sheets are entered on a smaller (5-inch by 3-inch) sheet, which is sent direct to the bureau. This information also is incorporated in the bureau and the National Central Library copies.

To summarize the advantages of the sheaf form for union catalogues we find:

(a) That the material for 1,000,000 entries (sheets, binders, and cases to hold the binders) costs £807, as compared with £1,477 in the case of a card catalogue (cards, cabinets, and guides).

(b) That 1,000,000 entries occupy a floor space of 36 square feet as compared with 101 square feet in the case of cards.

(c) That at approximately the same cost for labour four copies of the catalogue can be made, with a result that compilation is quicker and easier, and that a national as well as a regional catalogue can be compiled.

The third form of catalogue, that is printed or cyclostyled books, is the easiest to handle, occupies little space, and can be produced in as large a quantity as may be necessary; but it is expensive if printed, represents a good deal of additional work seeing it through the press, and cannot be kept up to date.

The approximate number of entries (including duplicates in some cases) in the union catalogues at the end of 1936 was:

At the National Central Library:

National Union Catalogue	545,000
Outlier Libraries	170,000
University Periodicals	100,000
London Public Libraries (a great many of these are duplicates)	1,345,000
South-Eastern Region	115,000
	2,275,000

Brought forward		2,275,000
In Wales:		
Welsh Regional Catalogues ..		573,000
In the other Regional Bureaux:		
Northern Region	298,000	
West Midland Region	180,000	
East Midland Region	80,000	
North-Western Region ..	123,000	
		681,000
Grand total, including many duplicate entries		3,529,000

The more important union catalogues, other than those already referred to and those which are published in printed or cyclostyled form, are:

(*a*) The Oxford inter-collegiate catalogue of books printed before 1641, compiled by Mr. G. R. Driver and Mr. S. Gibson. The method of compilation is to have the required entries typed from the college catalogue in two copies, one being retained by the college and the other cut up, mounted on cards, and made accessible in the Bodleian Library. By the end of 1935 nearly all the entries had been received, the total number being over 70,000. It is probable that when this material is fully edited the catalogue will be printed.

(*b*) The Cambridge inter-collegiate catalogue of books printed abroad, excluding English books, from 1501 to 1600, which is being compiled by Mr. H. M.

Adams. So far entries from four colleges and about half those from a fifth have been incorporated. It is estimated that the total number of entries will be about 30,000, and it is hoped that the catalogue will be published.

(c) A union catalogue of books on Scottish local history, consisting at present of about 4,000 entries supplied by the librarians of seventeen of the thirty county libraries in Scotland. The catalogue, which is housed at the Scottish Central Library for Students, is now arranged under authors' names, but it is hoped that when it is more complete it will have additional entries under places and under subjects.

(d) A union index of architectural drawings, engravings, etc. (not photographs or illustrations in books), of buildings erected before 1830, which is being compiled by the Architectural Graphic Records Committee. This index, which is housed in the Library of the Royal Institute of British Architects, is on cards, which are arranged topographically. By the end of 1936 over 11,000 drawings in twenty-four London libraries had been indexed. A great deal of work has still to be done and the Committee would welcome the assistance of more voluntary helpers. The Committee would also welcome gifts of any lists of architectural and topographical drawings, which should be sent to the Committee, care of the Librarian, Royal Institute of British Architects, 66 Portland Place, London, W.1.

Oxford is responsible for what appears to be the earliest printed union catalogue: the *Provisional catalogue of transactions of societies, periodicals, and memoirs available for the use of professors and of students*,[1] compiled by Mr. H. W. Acland, issued by the Radcliffe Library in 1866. This catalogue is a union catalogue to a limited extent only, as it gives locations in only three rather closely associated libraries: the Radcliffe, the Bodleian, and that of the Ashmolean Society. The first edition contains entries for about 320 periodicals, and the fourth, and last, edition published in 1887, contains about 1,200 entries. In the preface to the second edition it is stated that the Radcliffe Library "has been used by persons of either sex, by residents in the city and in the county, as well as by members of the university": an interesting early example of a broadminded library policy.

The next example of a printed union catalogue to be issued in the British Isles appears to be the *List of current scientific serial publications in the principal libraries of Manchester*,[2] compiled by Mr. C. W. E. Leigh and issued in 1898. In 1908 the Royal Society of London issued the first volume of the Subject Index[3] to their *Catalogue of Scientific Papers*. Each volume of the Index has a list of from 700 to 1,261 periodicals with locations in from twenty-four to thirty British libraries. In the following year a *Classified catalogue of the works on architecture and the allied arts in the*

[1] Bibliography, No. 97.   [2] Ibid., No. 98.   [3] Ibid., No. 99.

principal libraries of Manchester and Salford,[1] compiled by Dr. H. Guppy and Mr. G. Vine, was issued. This was followed in 1911 by the *List of medical periodicals preserved in the libraries of Ireland*,[2] compiled by Mr. R. Phelps. The pioneers of union catalogues covering a wider field were the Mathematical Association, who in 1913 issued a *Catalogue of current mathematical journals*,[3] under the editorship of Mr. W. J. Greenstreet. This catalogue listed 182 periodicals, with location references to forty-three libraries in the British Isles and six in South Africa. Although the main object of this catalogue was to show where sets of periodicals might be consulted, it led indirectly to a certain amount of lending, and may thus, perhaps, be looked upon as one of the earliest pieces of practical library co-operation.

The most important recent printed catalogues are:

(*a*) *A short-title catalogue of books printed in England, Scotland, and Ireland, and of English books printed abroad, 1475–1640*. Compiled by Dr. A. W. Pollard and Mr. G. R. Redgrave. 1926. This catalogue contains entries for 26,143 books, with locations in 153 libraries and private collections, mostly in the British Isles but a few in the United States of America. The aim of the catalogue is to give abridged entries of all books, printed before 1641, in whatever language, printed in England, Wales, Scotland, and Ireland, and all books in English wherever printed, also Latin service-

[1] Bibliography, No. 100.   [2] Ibid., No. 101.   [3] Ibid., No. 103.

UNION CATALOGUES

books, wherever printed, if for use in England and Scotland, copies of which exist at the British Museum, the Bodleian, the Cambridge University Library, and the Henry E. Huntington Library, California, supplemented by additions from nearly 150 other collections.

(b) *A world list of scientific periodicals published in the year 1900–1933.* Second edition, 1934. This list is one of the first importance to scientists and librarians. It contains entries for 24,029 sets of periodicals published during the years 1900–1933. Location references are given to 44 libraries in London and 143 in the provinces, a total of 187.

(c) *Union catalogue of the periodical publications in the university libraries of the British Isles.* Compiled on behalf of the Joint Standing Committee on Library Co-operation. 1937. This catalogue contains a list of all the periodicals, irrespective of date or subject, in all the university libraries, with the exception of those already included in the *World list of scientific periodicals*. 23,115 different periodicals are included, with details of the holdings of 110 libraries and fairly full bibliographical details. Including cross-references the total number of entries is about 55,000.

It is interesting to note how much useful "union cataloguing" is now done by some of the compilers of bibliographies, who thus often add materially to the value of their work. A few such books are given in numbers 102, 105, 107, 111, 116, 117, 119, 120, and 121 of the Bibliography.

CHAPTER X

HOW IT ALL WORKS

THIS short chapter gives a summary of the way in which an individual reader obtains a book through the national library service, as outlined in the previous chapters. The procedure is as follows:

(1) The reader asks at his "local" library for the book he wants. His local library may be an urban library, a county library, a university library, a special library, or the library of a learned institution of which he is a member.

(2) If the local library does not possess a copy of the book, and is not able to buy one, the librarian fills in an application form similar to the one shown on page 68. If his library is a member of a regional system he sends the form to his regional bureau.

If the local library is not a member of a regional system, the form is sent direct to the National Central Library, or in the case of Scotland and Ireland, to the Scottish Central Library for Students or the Irish Central Library for Students respectively.

(3) On receipt of the application form the staff at the regional bureau look the book up in their

HOW IT ALL WORKS

union catalogue, and if a copy is shown as being in any library in the regional area the application form is sent to that library, and the book is sent direct to the borrowing library, or in the case of a county library, to the reader's address.

(4) If no copy of the book is in the regional union catalogue the application form is sent direct to the National Central Library.

(5) The National Central Library tries to supply the book in one of the following ways:

   (*a*) From its own shelves;
   (*b*) By buying a copy;
   (*c*) By borrowing a copy from one of its outlier libraries;
   (*d*) By obtaining a copy through one of the other regional bureaux;
   (*e*) In exceptional cases, by borrowing a copy from a foreign library through the appropriate national centre.

At the end of 1936 the approximate total number of books available through the National Central Library, apart from those which might be obtained from foreign libraries, was as follows:

National Central Library's own stock	140,000
Special outlier libraries	2,657,000
Urban and county libraries in the regional systems	11,165,000
University libraries[1]	6,800,000[2]
Total	20,762,000

[1] In the case of one or two libraries the lending of books is restricted to other university libraries in the British Isles or abroad.

[2] This figure excludes the books in the Bodleian Library, Oxford; Cambridge University Library; the Library of Trinity College, Dublin; and a few Oxford and Cambridge college libraries which do not normally lend books to other libraries.

CHAPTER XI

POSSIBLE FUTURE DEVELOPMENTS

SINCE the foundation of the National Central Library twenty years ago the policy of its Trustees has been to meet, and not to create, a demand. This policy will always be followed, and as fresh demands arise from the libraries of the British Isles the Trustees will, so far as their financial resources allow, see that the Library gives such assistance as may be required from a national centre. What are these demands likely to be, and in what directions may the National Central Library and the regional systems be called upon to assist in promoting the efficiency of the national library service?

It is generally felt that as soon as the National Central Library is in a financial position to do so, it can render a most useful service by acting as a national reserve to which libraries of all types can transfer books—still useful, but no longer in frequent demand locally—which at present have to be discarded or left to occupy shelf space urgently needed for other more frequently used books. Almost all over the country there are libraries housing the same out-of-date books and sets of periodicals. The local demand is negligible, but the librarians realize that there is always a potential demand and, rightly, hesitate to get rid of such books.

Already the National Central Library has been able to take about 50,000 books of this nature. When this can be done on a larger scale hundreds of libraries will safely be able to get rid of many of their older books, having first ascertained that there is a copy at the National Central Library available on loan at any time. The aggregate saving of shelf space obtained in this way would be tremendous.

Those inexperienced in the details of inter-library lending may wonder whether it is worth while for the national centre to house books which are so out-of-date that the local libraries are glad to get rid of them. It has been found, over and over again, that it is the out-of-date book, which many libraries possessed at one time but have since discarded, that is the most difficult to get. The experience of many of the public outlier libraries is that most of the books they are able to supply at the request of the National Central Library are those which have long since been transferred to their "reserve" or "dormant" stock. There are few books which are not wanted at some time, not often enough to give them a place in every or any local library, but often enough fully to justify their inclusion in a national centre upon which all libraries can draw.

As early as 1896, Mr. E. Axon wrote, in an article entitled "Weeding out":[1]

---

[1] *The Library*, vol. 8, p. 264.

"The Free Reference Library, Manchester, contains over one hundred thousand volumes. So large a collection naturally entails the provision of a very considerable amount of shelf space, and in spite of very large additions, in recent years, to the shelving, the present building is getting inadequate. . . . With the object of saving space it has been thought desirable to 'weed out' the collection. . . . The difficulty of doing this will be apparent to all librarians. Every-day experience shows that the most out-of-the-way books often contain the precise information the reader wants, and that it is impossible to say with certainty that such a book is worthless and such a book is worth keeping. The occasional importance of old books is shown by a recent law case, in which the most important evidence, evidence which settled the case, was yielded by a treatise on photography which everyone would have said was absolutely out of date and useless."

Mr. J. P. Lamb, in an article on "Modern library organization,"[1] said in 1932,

"The great public reference libraries, instituted when they were practically the only libraries of their kind in the country, are now faced with such formidable competition that a careful examination of their function is surely called for. University and specialized libraries have helped to make a great deal of their work redundant, and the establishment of the National Central Library as the centre of a national book service is making it less necessary for them to stock the wide range of books many of them now carry at the cost of the virtual starvation of the lending libraries. The cost of housing, cataloguing, binding, and

[1] *Library Assistant*, vol. 25, pp. 248-253.

cleaning these vast accumulations of books is a charge which should be carefully considered."

Mr. Lamb again wrote, in 1935, in an article entitled "The efficient library in operation,"[1] "Great numbers of books are so rarely used, and the need there is for them is so seldom present, that it might be a sounder policy for the great city libraries to present large numbers of their Reference Books to the National Central Library. They would still be able to use them, whilst offering this privilege to others, and at the same time save themselves a great deal of expense in establishment charges and building costs."

Writing on the same subject in 1935, Mr. W. Hynes, at a meeting of the London and Home Counties Branch of the Library Association,[2] said,

"One can suggest that issue-value may well determine whether a book deserves shelf space in the local library, where space is so often at a premium, the book with reader-value which is seldom needed being sent to a central or regional repository and drawn therefrom when required. There is, of course, in the real sense no such central repository except the National Central Library, but it is not impossible with the development of regional bureaux, and as a result of the experience now being gained in their management, that such central repositories will eventually be found necessary. A central collection of standard but seldom called-for books would have obvious advantages. It would lessen the delay in searching for copies throughout the region, especially in those areas where a union catalogue is still incomplete. It would reduce expense in postages and time and clerical work for the harassed librarian, but

[1] *Library Association Record*, 4th series, vol. 2, pp. 421–427.
[2] Bibliography, No. 3.

above all it would enable him to dispense with many bulky volumes that at present he feels he must keep in view of possible rare demands."

Another possible useful development in the work of the National Central Library is that of acting as a centre for the exchange of duplicate or not wanted periodicals and books, limited, of course, to books which are worth while. Already the Library is doing a little in this way, it having been the channel through which 1,636 volumes were given to sixty-seven libraries during the year 1936.

Co-operation in book purchase is another possible development in regional co-operation. For a good many years much useful work in this direction has been done by small groups of neighbouring public libraries, and in several cases by the local public and university libraries. There would appear to be no reason why this should not be extended to larger groups, such as the groups represented by the regional systems. Such co-operation might take the form of mutual agreement in regard to the purchase of individual expensive or highly specialized books, or its nature might be that of a series of libraries each taking responsibility for building up a collection of books on some special subject, say one connected with a local industry or a celebrity associated with the town. Mr. L. R. McColvin's article, "Specialization and information,"[1] is of special interest in this connection.

[1] Bibliography, No. 10.

There can be little doubt that now that the principle of co-operation in the lending of books has been accepted, other forms of co-operation between libraries of all types—possibly some of those outlined in this chapter—will be introduced. There is much useful work still to be done, but it is to be hoped that before any new step is taken it will be given the most exhaustive consideration as the only way of avoiding wasteful effort.

APPENDIX

PROCEDURE FOR BORROWING BOOKS THROUGH REGIONAL LIBRARY BUREAUX

As the successful and harmonious working of the regional systems must depend upon a uniform procedure, it is hoped that all concerned will adhere to the following general rules.

1. **NORMAL PROCEDURE**
    (a) The reader will apply to his local library.
    (b) The library will apply to the Regional Bureau.
    (c) The Regional Bureau will consult the union catalogue and forward the application to:—
       (*a*) a library in the Region containing a copy of the book, or
       (*b*) the National Central Library, if the book is not available in the Region.
    (d) The National Central Library will deal with the application in the following order:—
       (*a*) supply the book from its own shelves;
       (*b*) buy a copy;
       (*c*) obtain it from an outlier library;
       (*d*) apply to other regional bureaux;
       (*e*) in exceptional cases, apply to one or more of the national centres for bibliographical information abroad.
    (e) If the book required can be lent, it will be sent by the lending library direct to the borrowing library, or, AT THE REQUEST OF A COUNTY LIBRARIAN ONLY, to the address of the borrower.

2. EXCEPTIONAL PROCEDURE

In urgent cases, when it is known with certainty that a book required is not in, or cannot be lent from, any library in the Region, the application may be sent direct to the National Central Library; but the reason for its being sent direct must be stated on the back of the application form. In other than urgent cases the normal procedure must be followed.

3. PERIOD FOR LOAN OF BOOKS

(a) The normal period for the loan of a book is fourteen days.
(b) Should a book be wanted for a longer period, arrangements for an extension must be made between the borrowing and the lending libraries.
(c) After consultation with the borrowing library, a lending library may issue a book for a shorter period if it cannot be spared for fourteen days.
(d) Should a lending library request the return of a book before it is due back, the borrowing library must comply with such a request as promptly as possible.

4. BOOKS LENT FROM REFERENCE DEPARTMENTS OF LIBRARIES

Books issued from the Reference Department of a library are, normally, for use only on the premises of another library. Books issued from the Lending Department of a library are, normally, available for home reading.

5. BOOKS FOR HOME READING

If a book is required for home reading only (i.e. if the reader would be unable to consult it in his local library) the application must be initialled in the space indicated on the form.

6. ARTICLES IN PERIODICALS

When the work required consists of an article in a periodical, the name of the author and the title of the article should be given, in addition to the title of the periodical and the number and date of the volume, as it is sometimes possible to obtain offprints when the complete volume is not available.

7. CONDITIONS OF SPECIAL LOANS

(a) When asked to lend a book of special value, a library may impose special conditions as to insurance, etc. Before such a book is sent the borrowing library shall be asked whether it is willing to accept the terms imposed.

(b) A borrowing library should be informed, before a book is despatched, if the total cost of transport both ways would exceed five shillings.

8. RIGHT TO REFUSE THE LOAN OF A BOOK

A library shall be at liberty to refuse to lend any particular book.

9. PURCHASE OF BOOKS IN FREQUENT DEMAND

When a library has to borrow the same book frequently, it is expected that an endeavour will be made by the borrowing library to purchase a copy for its own stock.

10. FORMS OF APPLICATION

(a) Each application shall be made on one of the official forms of application, A SEPARATE FORM BEING USED FOR EACH BOOK REQUIRED.
(b) Forms may be sent in a tucked-in envelope for one halfpenny.
(c) Copies of the official form of application may be obtained free of charge on application to the Regional Bureau.

11. METHOD OF DEALING WITH APPLICATION FORMS

(a) If the Regional Bureau locates a copy of a book required, the application form will be forwarded to the library containing the copy. If no copy available for loan can be located within the Region, the form will be forwarded to the National Central Library.
(b) If the library to which the form is forwarded is able to lend the book, the librarian will enter the date on which the book is sent and retain the form as a record.
(c) If the library to which the form is forwarded is unable to lend the book, the stamp of the library will be put on the back of the form, which will be returned at once to the Regional Bureau.
(d) If, at the time at which an application is received, a library is unable to lend the book, but is willing for it to be consulted on its own premises, the form will be returned to the Regional Bureau, with a note on the back saying that the book may be consulted.

12. ACKNOWLEDGMENT OF RECEIPT OF A BOOK

A lending library should provide and send a receipt form with each book despatched. This form must be signed and returned direct to the lending library IMMEDIATELY UPON THE RECEIPT OF THE BOOK BY THE BORROWING LIBRARY.

13. POSTAGE ON BOOKS

The cost of postage should be refunded direct to the lending library IMMEDIATELY UPON THE RECEIPT OF THE BOOK BY THE BORROWING LIBRARY.

14. RETURN OF BOOKS TO LENDING LIBRARIES

(a) All books returned to a lending library must be sent carriage paid by the borrowing library.

(b) ALL BOOKS MUST BE CAREFULLY PACKED, SEVERAL LAYERS OF PAPER OR CARDBOARD BEING USED.

(c) When a book which has been borrowed is returned to the lending library, the receipt form will be endorsed "Cancelled," and returned to the borrowing library.

15. RESPONSIBILITY FOR BOOKS ON LOAN

(a) A borrowing library shall be responsible for any book lent, from the time it leaves the lending library until it is received by the lending library. The borrowing library shall pay to the lending library the full value of any loss or damage.

(b) If a borrowing library receives a damaged or imperfect book, it must at once notify the lending library.

16. PROCEDURE IN CASE OF INFECTIOUS DISEASE

Should any infectious or contagious disease occur in a house containing a book belonging to another library, the librarian of the lending library shall at once be notified, and the book shall not be returned until instructions have been received from him.

BIBLIOGRAPHY

I. GENERAL

1. BRADLEY (L. J. H.) and BRISCOE (W. A.). Co-operation with public libraries.
   Library Association Record. 3rd Series. Vol. 3, 1933, pp. xvii-xx.
   Deals with co-operation between university and public libraries.

1A. BROWN (J. D.). Manual of library economy. Fifth edition by W. C. Berwick Sayers, 1937. Chapter 36. A national library service.

2. DOUBLEDAY (W. E.), *Editor*. A primer of librarianship. 1931. Chapter 14. Library co-operation and the National Central Library, by L. Newcombe.

3. HYNES (W.). Revision of stock.
   Library Association Record. 4th Series. Vol. 2, 1935, pp. 304–309.
   The author emphasizes the value of a central repository for little used books.
   See pages 124 and 146.

4. KENYON (SIR FREDERIC G.). The modern library.
   The Times Literary Supplement. Vol. 34, 1935, pp. 181–182.
   This article reviews the progress made in the public library service, mainly through the National Central Library and the regional systems, since the publication of the Report of the Departmental Committee on Public Libraries in 1927.

5. KEOGH (CHRISTINA A.). Library co-operation in practice.
   Journal of the Library Association of Ireland. Vol. 4, 1934, pp. 77–87.

6. KIRBY (S.). Co-operation: a suggestion.
Library Assistant. Vol. 5, 1907, pp. 266–269.
See page 35.

7. LAMB (J. P.). The Sheffield experiment: how it is succeeding.
Report of the Twelfth Conference of the Association of Special Libraries and Information Bureaux. 1935, pp. 97–102.
See page 103.

8. LEIPPRAND (E.). Kooperationsbestrebungen im modernen englischen Bibliothekswesen.
Zentralblatt für Bibliothekswesen. Jahrgang 48, 1931, pp. 601–627.
This important article gives a full survey of all aspects of library co-operation in the British Isles. Bibliography.

9. MCCOLVIN (L. R.). The future of public libraries.
Library Review. Vol. 3, 1932, pp. 231–236.
The author says that co-operation is essential and that ultimately all libraries must help one another. He says also that once readers realize the possibility of borrowing, the usefulness of the service will increase rapidly. He thinks that co-operation in the supply of information will also have to come.

10. ——— Specialization and information.
Library Review. Vol. 4, 1934, pp. 329–336.
The author suggests that in order that the smaller libraries may be in a position to contribute their share in a general system of co-operation they should specialize, and that this specialization should be organized on a national scale. He also emphasizes the need for a national information service.

11. ——— Library co-operation in Great Britain.
Bulletin of the American Library Association. Vol. 30, 1936, pp. 914–918.

12. MITCHELL (J. M.). County Libraries.
Conference on libraries in Wales and Monmouthshire.

Report of the Proceedings. 1925, pp. 19–26.
This paper deals with general library co-operation, co-operative book-buying, and union catalogues. In conclusion it suggests that Wales might be the first area in the British Isles to adopt a regional system.

13. MITCHELL (J. M.) An address to the American Library Association Conference, 1932.
Library Review. Vol. 3, 1932, pp. 321–331.
One of the subjects dealt with in this address is the development of regional and other co-operation in the British Isles.

14. NEWCOMBE (L.). Intercommunication between special libraries.
Report of the Third Conference of the Association of Special Libraries and Information Bureaux. 1926, pp. 11–19.
This paper suggests how ASLIB, the National Central Library, and other bodies might work in closer co-operation. It concludes with a plan for a central building to house all associations interested in library matters. It is of interest to note that five of the seven bodies mentioned are now housed in the Malet Place block of buildings.

15. ——— The library service of Great Britain.
World Conference on Adult Education, Cambridge, 1929, pp. 273–279.
One of a series of international papers on "Libraries and adult education."

16. ——— Inter-library loans in Great Britain.
The South Indian Teacher. Vol. 3, 1931, pp. 181–187.
This paper, written for the First All Asia Educational Conference in 1930, gives information about the various methods of co-operation in the British Isles and the work of the National Central Library. It led to the adoption of a resolution "requesting the Inter-University Board of India to bring into operation a scheme of inter-university library loan of books and periodicals."

17. PAFFORD (J. H. P.). Library co-operation: an outline of objects, methods, and achievements.
Library Assistant. Vol. 26, 1933, pp. 109–118 and 137–140.

18. ——— Library co-operation in Europe. 1935.
This is the only book giving a general survey of the system of co-operation in European countries. Part 1 deals with general principles and practice, and Part 2 with the existing systems of co-operation. Bibliography of 293 items.

19. SELLICK (E.). Regionalization and the Reference Library.
Library Assistant. Vol. 28, 1935, pp. 58–65.

20. WARNER (J.). Reference library methods. 1928.
Chapter 11, Inter-library loans; and Chapter 12, Other means of co-operation.

21. WRIGHT (R.). Co-operation and county libraries.
Carnegie United Kingdom Trust, County Library Conference, 1924. Report of the proceedings. pp. 83–99.

22. PUBLIC LIBRARIES COMMITTEE. Report on public libraries in England and Wales. H.M. Stationery Office. 1927. Cmd. 2868.
——— [A reprint, without the statistical tables, was published in 1935.]
This Report is one of the first importance, dealing with all aspects of the public library movement in England and Wales. Its particular reference to the subject of this book is in Chapter 5, "An organized national service." See page 54.

23. The Central Library for Students. 1st (–14th) annual report of the Library Committee. 1916–17 to 1929–30.
Continued as
The National Central Library. 15th (16th, etc.) annual report of the Executive Committee. 1930–31, etc.
The twelfth and following reports contain the most

BIBLIOGRAPHY 159

complete summaries of the progress made during the year of the outlier library system, the regional library systems, international lending, and union catalogues.

24. The Year's Work in Librarianship. Vol. 1, *etc.*, 1928, *etc.* Edited for the Library Association. 1929, *etc.*
An important source for information on national and international library co-operation. Bibliography.

25. Library Association. Small municipal libraries: a manual of modern method. Second edition, 1934. Chapter 4, Co-operation of stock.
A short bibliography.

26. Proceedings of the Scottish Library Conference, held at Dunblane, 1931.
The main proceedings of this Conference dealt with co-operation between the Scottish libraries. Four resolutions were adopted, three dealing with co-operation between urban and county authorities, and the fourth recommending that there should be a National Central Library for Scotland on the lines of the National Central Library in London.

27. Co-operation between public libraries in Northern Ireland.
The Librarian. Vol. 17, 1928, pp. 191–193.

28. Government of Northern Ireland. Report of the Departmental Committee on Libraries in Northern Ireland. Belfast. H.M. Stationery Office. 1929. Cmd. 101.
The main recommendations of the Committee are dealt with on page 47.

II. HISTORICAL

29. BAKER (E. A.). Some recent developments of library co-operation.
Library Association Record. Vol. 10, 1908, pp. 660–677; Discussion, pp. 593–6.
Bibliography.

30. C. (J. D.). Co-operation between municipal and county libraries.
   The Librarian, Vol. 17, 1928, pp. 147–150.
   The author suggests that a serious hindrance to any co-operative schemes on a large scale is likely to be the lack of a central co-ordinating body.

31. MITCHELL (J. M.). The public library system of Great Britain and Ireland. 1921–23. Carnegie United Kingdom Trust. 1924.
   See page 45.

32. PANIZZI (SIR ANTHONY). On the collection of printed books at the British Museum, its increase and arrangement. Appendix I: On the advantages and disadvantages of lending books from public libraries. [Report to the Trustees.] [1845.]
   See page 32.

33. PHILIP (A. J.). A reference library for London.
   The Contemporary Review. Vol. 102, 1912, pp. 388–396.
   See page 39.

34. PITT (S. A.). Possible co-operation in reference library work.
   Library Association Record. Vol. 15, 1913, pp. 408–412.
   See page 41.

35. POLLARD (A. W.). A national lending library for students.
   The Library. 3rd Series. Vol. 4, 1913, pp. 353–368.
   See page 41.

36. ⸺ The Panizzi Club.
   The Library. 3rd Series. Vol. 5, 1914, pp. 95–102.
   See page 43.

37. ⸺ On getting to work: part of a paper read before the Panizzi Club, June 24, 1914.
   The Library. 3rd Series. Vol. 5, 1914, pp. 325–336.
   See page 44.

38. POWELL (W.). Interlibrary loans in Great Britain.
In James A. McMillen's "Selected articles on interlibrary loans." 1928, pp. 25–32.
This article shows how little was being done in 1928, though it fails to note the outlier libraries of the National Central Library, thirty-six of which had lent 1,606 books during the previous year.

39. SAVAGE (E. A.). Memorandum on the organization of library exchange areas.
Library Association Record. Vol. 19, 1917, pp. 328–9.
This memorandum outlines a scheme for lending books to other libraries from the Birmingham and Coventry Public Libraries.
See page 44.

40. WEBB (SIDNEY). The library service of London: its co-ordination, development, and education.
Library Association Record. Vol. 4, 1902, pp. 193–203, 231–236.
See page 34.

41. "Some London Librarians." Our Public Libraries.
Contemporary Review. Vol. 104, 1913, pp. 250–258.
See page 40.

III. THE NATIONAL CENTRAL LIBRARY

See also number 22.

Other articles on the work of the National Central Library have appeared in many periodicals, too numerous to detail here. The information in these articles is mostly included in the articles in this bibliography.

42. COTTON (W. E. C.) The Scottish Central Library for Students.
County Library Conference, 1926. Report of proceedings, pp. 102–105.

43. DOUGLAS (F. E.). The National Central Library: its work and progress.
   The Journal of Adult Education. Vol. 6, 1934, pp. 458-462.

44. KEOGH (CHRISTINA A.). The Irish Central Library for Students.
   County Library Conference, 1926. Report of proceedings, pp. 105-109.

45. ———— The Irish Central Library for Students.
   Journal of the Library Association of Ireland. Vol. 2, 1932, pp. 80-82.

46. NEWCOMBE (L.). The Central Library for Students and the County Libraries.
   County Library Conference. 1926. Report of proceedings, pp. 92-102.

47. ———— The future of the Central Library for Students.
   Proceedings of the Fiftieth Anniversary Conference of the Library Association. 1927, pp. 169-194.
   This paper outlines the foundation and present position of the Central Library for Students and then goes on to suggest various ways in which the Library might assist other libraries. The discussion following the paper emphasises the need of a central store for little used, but still useful, books. This paper led to the addition of the first two urban libraries (Brighton and Croydon) and the first county library (Warwickshire) to the group of outlier libraries.

48. ———— A national book pool.
   Library Review. Vol. 1, 1927, pp. 10-13.
   Outlines the national service available (in 1927) to local readers.

49. ———— The National Central Library and its work.
   Report of the Proceedings of the Eleventh Annual Conference of Library Authorities in Wales and Monmouthshire. 1936, pp. 38-46.

BIBLIOGRAPHY 163

50. PAFFORD (J. H. P.). Library co-operation in Europe.
    1935, Chapter 9.
    Bibliography of 39 items.

51. POLLARD (A. W.). The Central Library for Students.
    Library Association Record. Vol. 19, 1917, pp. 372-378.
    See page 53.

52. PREDEEK (A.). Das moderne englische Bibliothekswesen.
    1933, Chapter 5. Co-operation und die National
    Central Library.
    Bibliography of 119 items.

53. The Central Library for Students. 1st (-14th) annual
    report of the Library Committee. 1916-17 to 1929-30.
    Continued as
    The National Central Library. 15th (16th, etc.) annual
    report of the Executive Committee. 1930-31, etc.
    The twelfth and following reports contain the most complete summaries of the progress made during the year of the outlier library system, the regional library systems, international lending, and union catalogues.

54. Ministry of Reconstruction. Third interim report of the Adult Education Committee. Libraries and museums. H.M. Stationery Office. 1919. Cmd. 9237.
    See page 50.

55. Royal Commission on National Museums and Galleries. Final Report, Part 1. H.M. Stationery Office. 1929. Cmd. 3401. Pp. 63-67 and 77-78.
    ——— Oral evidence, memoranda, and appendices. Pp. 63-85, 124-126, and 136-139.
    This Report deals with the Central Library for Students (now the National Central Library) as a State institution. As a result of the Report the Library received its first annual grant from the national Exchequer. For details see page 58.

56. The National Central Library: its work and needs. 1936.
This pamphlet, issued by the National Central Library, outlines the main functions of the Library.

IV. THE OUTLIER LIBRARIES

See also number 23.

57. GORRIE (T.). Special libraries: the problem of co-operation with the public service.
Report of the Second Conference of the Association of Special Libraries and Information Bureaux. 1925, pp. 60–64.
The author, speaking as the representative of the Carnegie United Kingdom Trustees, outlines the outlier library policy of the Trustees.

58. HEADICAR (B. M.). Co-operation between libraries, Government departments, political societies, and other special institutions.
Report of the Fourth Conference of the Association of Special Libraries and Information Bureaux. 1927, pp. 30–33.
The author advocates the lending of books by special libraries to the public libraries, and suggests other ways in which libraries of various types might assist one another.

59. HYSLOP (A. B.). The "Outlier" policy of the Carnegie United Kingdom Trust.
Report of the Third Conference of the Association of Special Libraries and Information Bureaux. 1926, pp. 7–10.
The author outlines the origin and growth of the outlier library system and discusses possible difficulties.

60. TWENTYMAN (A. E.) and NEWCOMBE (L.). The Report of the Public Libraries Committee of the Board of

Education, with particular reference to the place of the special library in a national information service.
Report of the Fourth Conference of the Association of Special Libraries and Information Bureaux. 1927, pp. 21–27.

V. THE REGIONAL LIBRARY SYSTEMS

See also numbers 23, 89, 94.

61. BURGESS (L. A.). Co-operation again.
    Library Assistant. Vol. 27, 1934, pp. 60–66 and 129–130.
    This article is a sequel to the articles by C. Sexton and M. C. Pottinger. See Nos. 67 and 65.

62. DAVIES (W. LLEWELYN). A federal union of libraries in Wales.
    The Journal of the Welsh Bibliographical Society. Vol. 3, 1931, pp. 311–323.
    The author suggests that the solution of the problems of the small library is co-operation on a national scale. He recommends the adoption of a regional system for Wales.

63. DOUBLEDAY (W. E.). A manual of library routine. 1933, pp. 257–268.
    A short bibliography. Deals mainly with the regional systems and the National Central Library.

64. DOWIE (MARGARET L.). Possible developments in the Scottish library service, with special reference to regional co-operation.
    Library Association Record. 3rd Series. Vol. 3, 1933, pp. 148–151.

65. POTTINGER (M. C.). Co-operation in fact.
    Library Assistant. Vol. 26, 1933, pp. 202–209 and 240–242.
    This article is a sequel to C. Sexton's article. See No. 67.

66. ROBERTS (A. D.). Regional library bureaux: summary of progress.

The Library World. Vol. 37, 1934–35, pp. 131–134 and 180–183.
The first part of this article summarizes the existing literature, official and otherwise. In the second part the author discusses possible developments. Among other things he suggests that "Government grants to support the National Central Library and the Regional Bureaux would be equivalent to a flat rate over the whole of the country."

67. SEXTON (C.). Co-operation in practice.
Library Assistant. Vol. 26, 1933, pp. 175–180.
See also numbers 61 and 65.

68. TOMBLIN (JANET). Sidelights on library book selection.
Library Association Record. 4th Series. Vol. 2, 1935, pp. 450–456.
This paper, by the editor of the union catalogue of the South Eastern Regional System, advocates other forms of co-operation, such as enquiry at the regional bureau before purchasing expensive or highly specialized books, as well as before withdrawing books, with a view to finding out what other copies, if any, are in other libraries. She also recommends specialization by each library in a region. A valuable paper in connection with possible future developments.

69. WRIGHT (R.). The work of the South Eastern Regional Library System.
Library Association Record. 4th Series. Vol. 1, 1934, pp. 209–213.

70. Public Libraries Committee. Report on public libraries in England and Wales. H.M. Stationery Office. 1927. Cmd. 2868.
[A reprint without the statistical tables, was published in 1935.]
This Report is one of the first importance, dealing with all aspects of the public library movement in England and Wales. Its particular reference to the subject of this book

BIBLIOGRAPHY

is in Chapter 5, "an organized national service." For details see page 84.

71. Library Association. Regional libraries in England. A report of the Committee of the County Libraries Section.
    Library Association Record. New Series. Vol. 6, 1928, pp. 243–251.
    This Report contains a map showing the suggested grouping of libraries. For details see page 85.

72. Conference on libraries in Wales and Monmouthshire. [1st etc.] Report of the proceedings. 1925, etc.
    These reports are of importance in connection with the establishment and development of the Welsh Regional Library System.

73. Welsh Branch of the Library Association. Publication No. 1. Library co-operation in Wales, by H. Farr and W. Williams; together with an address on inter-library loans by L. Newcombe. 1931.
    These articles are published also in the Report of the Proceedings of the Sixth Conference on Libraries in Wales and Monmouthshire, 1931. This publication is of interest in the early history of the Welsh Regional Library System.

74. Procedure for borrowing books through regional library bureaux. Second edition. 1934.
    This pamphlet, issued by the National Central Library in conjunction with the Regional Library Bureaux, is printed in full on pages 149 to 154.

75. The following reports of the Regional Library Committees:

    Northern, for the year 1931, etc.
    West Midland, for the year 1931, etc.
    Wales, for the year 1932, etc.
    South-Eastern, for the year 1934, etc
    East Midland, for the year 1935, etc.
    North-Western, for the year 1935, etc.
    Yorkshire, for the year 1935, etc.

VI. THE UNIVERSITY LIBRARIES

See also number 23.

76. OLDAKER (L. T.). The J.S.C.L.C. [Joint Standing Committee on Library Co-operation] Enquiry Office at Birmingham: a retrospect.
Library Association Record. 3rd Series. Vol. 2, 1932, pp. 118–123.
This article outlines the work of the Enquiry Office from the date of its foundation in 1923 until it was handed over to the National Central Library in 1931.

77. SANDBACH (F. E.). Inter-library lending.
Library Association Record. New Series. Vol. 3, 1925, pp. 230–241; Discussion, pp. viii–xi.

78. ——— Information on the work and aims of the Library Co-operation Committee and its Enquiry Office.
Report of the Second Conference of the Association of Special Libraries and Information Bureaux. 1925. pp. 186–187.

79. Association of University Teachers. Conference on Library Co-operation.
[Report of the Joint Standing Committee on Library Co-operation.] 1, etc. 1925, etc.

VII. THE LONDON LIBRARIES

See also numbers 23, 33, 40, 41, 93, 131.

80. BAKER (E. A.). The public library. 1924. Chapter 5. A national library service.
This chapter deals largely with possible co-operation between the libraries of London.

81. ESDAILE (A. J. K.). The unification of the library resources of London.
Report of the Fifth Conference of the Association of Special Libraries and Information Bureaux. 1928, pp. 65-72.
The author outlines a scheme by which both the public and the private libraries of London could co-operate, by inter-lending and in other ways.

82. INKSTER (L.) and BAKER (E. A.). Co-operative schemes for libraries in the London area.
Library Association Record. Vol. 11, 1909, pp. 9-16.

83. MCKILLOP (J.). The present position of London Municipal Libraries, with suggestions for increasing their efficiency.
Library Association Record. Vol. 8, 1906, pp. 625-635; Discussion, pp. 495-7.
See page 36.

84. STEWART (J. D.). Possibilities in the development of inter-library relations in London and the London area.
Library Association Record. New Series. Vol. 4, 1926. pp. 7-21.

VIII. INTERNATIONAL LENDING

See also number 23.

85. PAFFORD (J. H. P.). Library co-operation in Europe. 1935.
This is the only book giving a general survey of the systems of co-operation in European countries. Part 1 deals with general principles and practice, and Part 2 with the existing systems of co-operation. Bibliography of 293 items.

86. League of Nations. International Institute of Intellectual Co-operation. Committee of experts for the

establishment of an international co-ordination service of libraries. Reports. 1928.
Chapter 4, by Sir Frederic G. Kenyon, deals with the existing services in the British Isles.

87. League of Nations. Institut International de Coopération Intellectuelle. Guide des services nationaux de renseignements du prêt et des échanges internationaux. 2e édition. 1933.
This guide gives information about the national centres for the loan of books, with details of the conditions of loan.

IX. ARTICLES ON UNION CATALOGUES

87A. BERTHOLD (A.). Union catalogues; a selective bibliography. 1936.
This is the most complete bibliography (containing 356 annotated references) on union cataloguing in various parts of the world.

88. GIBSON (S.). Library co-operation in Oxford. Oxford Bibliographical Society: Proceedings and papers. Vol. 2, 1930, pp. 201–205.
See page 30.

89. MOORE (HILDA M.). The mechanism of regional cataloguing.
Library Association Record. 4th Series. Vol. 2, 1935, pp. 561–568.
The author bases her article on considerable experience as editor of the Northern regional catalogue. She deals fully with all the practical details connected with the compilation of a great union catalogue. A paper of the first importance to those about to undertake this work.

90. NEWCOMBE (L.). Union catalogues, national and regional: their preparation and utilization.
Report of the Thirteenth Conference of the Association

of Special Libraries and Information Bureaux. 1936. pp. 65–76.

91. PAFFORD (J. H. P.). Library co-operation in Europe. 1935, Chapter 4.
Deals with the theory and practice of union catalogues in the British Isles and abroad and shows how much successful and economic co-operation depends upon such catalogues. Bibliography.

92. POLLARD (A. W.). Future work on the short-title catalogue of English books, 1475–1640.
The Library. 4th Series. Vol. 8, 1928, pp. 377–394.

93. SMITH (F. SEYMOUR). The reference libraries of London: is a union catalogue a practicable proposition?
Report of the Fourth Conference of the Association of Special Libraries and Information Bureaux. 1927, pp. 34–39.
The author emphasizes the urgent need for a union catalogue of the London libraries and outlines practical working details for such a catalogue. This paper is of special interest as the one which led indirectly to the establishment of the London Public Libraries Union Catalogue, which in turn led to the introduction of an inter-lending system between the London Borough libraries. See pages 126 to 130.

94. TAYLOR (MARGARET S.). The Northern regional catalogue.
The Library Assistant. Vol. 25, 1932, pp. 147–154 and 182–183.
This paper is by the editor of the Northern union catalogue.

95. Towards union cataloguing.
Library Association Record. New Series. Vol. 7, 1929. Supplement, pp. 20–50 and viii–ix.
A series of papers read before the 52nd Annual Conference of the Library Association. 1. Social sciences, by B. M. Headicar; 2 (i) The information service of the Science Library, by S. C. Bradford; 2 (ii) The World List of Scientific Periodicals, by W. A. Smith; 3. In London and

172 LIBRARY CO-OPERATION

in the university libraries, by L. Newcombe; 4. In Wales, by J. Ballinger; 5. In Cornwall, by Miss W. M. Gayton; 6. The Mansfield, Worksop, Newark scheme, by A. Smith.

96. Oxford. Report on the inter-collegiate catalogue of early printed books [1st–5th reports]. 1931–35.
See page 135.

X. UNION CATALOGUES

96A. BERNARD (EDWARD). Catalogi librorum manuscriptorum Angliæ et Hiberniæ in unum collecti, cum indice alphabetico. Oxford, 1697.
This catalogue may perhaps be looked upon as the first British union catalogue. It contains many thousand entries of manuscripts in the Bodleian Library, the Oxford and Cambridge college libraries, cathedral libraries, and some private collections.

97. Oxford University. Radcliffe Library. Provisional catalogue of transactions of societies, periodicals, and memoirs available for the use of professors and students. [Compiled by H. W. Acland.] [1866.]
———— 2nd edition. 1871.
———— 3rd edition. 1876.
———— 4th edition. 1887.
See page 137.

98. Manchester Literary and Philosophical Society. List of the current scientific serial publications received by the principal libraries of Manchester. Compiled by Charles W. E. Leigh. 1898.
Contains references to 741 periodicals in nine libraries.

99. Royal Society of London. Catalogue of scientific papers 1800 to 1900. Subject index. Vols. 1–3, 1908–14.
Each volume has a list of from 700 to 1,261 periodicals with locations in from twenty-four to thirty British libraries.

BIBLIOGRAPHY

100. Joint Architectural Committee of Manchester. A classified catalogue of the works on architecture and the allied arts in the principal libraries of Manchester and Salford. . . . Edited by Henry Guppy and Guthrie Vine. 1909.
A very full catalogue of 310 pages giving locations of books in eleven libraries. The introduction claims that the book is "the first of its kind, with the exception of a few union lists of periodicals and incunabula, to be issued either in this country or abroad."

101. List of medical periodicals preserved in the libraries of Ireland. [1911.]
This list, compiled by R. Phelps, the librarian of the Royal College of Physicians of Ireland, gives locations in twelve libraries for about 284 periodicals.

102. JAGGARD (W.). Shakespeare bibliography. 1911.
Gives locations in twenty-one libraries in the British Isles and in seven foreign libraries.

103. [GREENSTREET (W. J.).] Catalogue of current mathematical journals, etc.: with the names of the libraries in which they may be found. Compiled for the Mathematical Association, London, 1913.
See page 138.

104. Union class list of the libraries of the Library and Library Assistants' Associations, 1913.

105. DUFF (E. G.). Fifteenth century English books. 1917.
Gives locations in many British libraries and private collections.

106. LEIPER (R. T.). Periodicals of medicine and the allied sciences in British libraries. 1923.
Gives locations in thirty-seven libraries in the British Isles.

107. HAWKES (A. J.). Lancashire printed books. 1925.
Gives locations for 1,055 books in twenty-seven libraries and private collections in the British Isles.

108. HEWITT (C. R.). Current medical periodicals of the British Empire.
The Medical Year Book, 1925. pp. 545–550.
A union list of British periodicals in the five principal medical libraries in London.

109. Current foreign and colonial periodicals in the Bodleian Library and in other Oxford libraries. 1925.
Gives locations for 2,275 periodicals in thirty-six libraries.

110. Gesamtkatalog der Wiegendrucke. 1925, etc.
This catalogue of books printed before the year 1500 contains location references to several hundred libraries throughout the world, including many in the British Isles.

111. BEALE (J. H.). A bibliography of early English law books. 1926.
Gives locations in eighteen British and seven American libraries.

112. POLLARD (A. W.) and REDGRAVE (G. R.). A short-title catalogue of books printed in England, Scotland, and Ireland, and of English books printed abroad, 1475–1640. 1926.
See page 138 and Bibliography No. 92.

112A. CRANE (R.S.) and KAYE (F.B.). A census of British newspapers and periodicals. 1620–1800. 1927.
Contains locations for 970 periodicals in 62 libraries in the United States of America; also a list of over 1,200 periodicals not found in American libraries. Bibliography of 56 items.

113. Literary and Philosophical Society of Newcastle-upon-Tyne. Union List of Periodicals.
Quarterly Record. Vol. 1, 1928, pp. 35–80.
A list of about 1,800 periodicals in eleven libraries in Newcastle. The entries consist only of a brief title followed by the names of libraries containing the periodicals.

114. National Library of Ireland. List of scientific and technical periodicals in Dublin libraries. 1929.

This list, running to 147 pages, gives the location of all the periodicals in eighteen libraries in Dublin.

115. List of books on the Ribble Valley in the Accrington, Blackburn, Burnley, and Preston Public Libraries. 1930.

116. PEDDIE (R. A.). Railway literature, 1556–1830. 1931.
Gives locations in twenty-eight libraries and private collections in the British Isles and sixteen in Europe and America.

117. ROBERTSON (J. D.). The evolution of clockwork. 1931.
The extensive bibliography on pages 289 to 348 contains locations in six libraries in London.

118. A London bibliography of the social sciences. Compiled under the direction of B. M. Headicar and C. Fuller. 1931–32, and supplements.
Gives locations in ten libraries in London.

119. COWLEY (J. D.). A bibliography of abridgements, digests, dictionaries, and indexes of English law to the year 1800. Selden Society. 1932.
This bibliography contains 330 books. Nearly all the references contain location marks showing where copies of the books are available in twenty-five libraries in the British Isles and America.

120. GOSS (C. W. F.). The London directories, 1677–1855: a bibliography. 1932.
Gives locations in eight libraries and private collections in London and one in Manchester.

121. HARRISON (F. M.). A bibliography of the works of John Bunyan. 1932.
Gives locations for all known copies in many libraries and private collections in the British Isles, Europe, and America.

122. A world list of scientific periodicals published in the years 1900–1933. 2nd edition. 1934.
See page 139.

176 LIBRARY CO-OPERATION

123. University Library, Cambridge. Select list of current English periodicals. 1934.
Gives locations in eleven libraries in Cambridge.

124. University Library, Cambridge. List of current foreign and colonial periodicals. 1934.
Gives locations in forty libraries in Cambridge.

125. Sheffield Public Libraries. Interchange of technical publications. Union list of scientific, technical, and commercial periodicals in the libraries of members of the Group Interchange System. 1934.
A cyclostyled list which, with additions issued from time to time, contains entries for many hundred periodicals in the principal libraries of Sheffield.

126. List of current periodicals and serials in Belfast libraries. Fourth edition. 1937.
This cyclostyled list, compiled by K. Povey, indexes about 1,370 current periodicals in 27 libraries in Belfast.

127. List of technical, scientific, and commercial periodicals taken by certain libraries in Manchester. Compiled by the Lancashire and Cheshire Branch of ASLIB. [1936.]
A cyclostyled list of forty-five pages giving locations in nine libraries.

128. Union catalogue of the periodical publications in the university libraries of the British Isles: with their respective holdings. Excluding titles in the "World List of Scientific Periodicals, 1934."
To be published in 1937.
See page 139.

XI. GUIDES TO MATERIAL

129. BAKER (E. A.). The uses of libraries. New [2nd] edition. 1930.
Bibliography.

130. NEWCOMBE (L.). The university and college libraries of Great Britain and Ireland. A guide to the material available for the research student. 1927.
Gives information about the special collections in the university and college libraries, with a note as to how the public may obtain access to them.

131. RYE (R. A.). The students' guide to the libraries of London. Third edition. 1927.
The most complete guide to the material in the university, special and public libraries of London. It explains how access to the libraries may be obtained by members of the public.

132. The ASLIB Directory: a guide to sources of specialized information in Great Britain and Ireland. Edited by G. F. Barwick. 1928.
This book, issued by the Association of Special Libraries and Information Bureaux, is the only complete guide to the library resources of the British Isles. The first portion (occupying 304 pages) contains references to special collections arranged under subject headings. Brief details of each collection are given, with a note of the library in which it is contained. The second portion (pages 305–410) consists of a list of the libraries referred to in the body of the book, arranged under the name of the towns in which they are located. This list gives the address of the library and brief information about the hours of opening and the possibilities of access to persons who are not members. The book concludes with an index to named collections.

133. The libraries, museums, and art galleries year book.
Contains a section giving details of collections on special subjects.

INDEX

Adult Education Committee, Report, 1919 50
Architectural drawings, union catalogue of 136
Association of Special Libraries and Information Bureaux 46
Axon, E., Points out danger of discarding little used books 144

Bibliography 155
Birmingham inter-lending scheme, 1917 44
Bond, E. A., Suggestions for co-operation in 1886 34
Book purchase, co-operation in 147
Books, central store for 36
British Museum, suggested lending of duplicates from 32

Cambridge inter-collegiate catalogue, 1501–1600 135
Carnegie United Kingdom Trust, Assistance given to the movement for co-operation 48
Central lending library—
    recommendations of the Adult Education Committee, 1919 50
    suggested establishment 39–41
Central Library for Students. *See* National Central Library [formerly Central Library for Students]
Central store for books 36, 145–146
Co-operation—
    foundation and development of. Chapter II
    future in hands of librarians 28
    need for an organized system. Chapter I
    pioneers of. Chapter II
    suggestions for in 1914 44
    systems of, other than the regional systems 101–103
Cotton des Houssayes, J. B., *Duties and qualifications of a librarian* 29
Coventry inter-lending scheme, 1917 44

Davies, E. Salter 48
Departmental Committee on Public Libraries, Recommendations of 54–57
Developments, possible future. Chapter XI
Duplicates, exchange of 147
Durie, John, *The reformed librarie-keeper* 18

Elgin and Kincardine, The Earl of 48
English books printed before 1641, union catalogue of 138

Form used when applying for the loan of a book 68

How it all works. Chapter X
Hulme, E. Wyndham 43
Hynes, W., Suggests central book repository 146
    suggests uses for union catalogues 124

Inter-library lending—
    first organized system 37
    what it does and does not mean 19
International library loans. Chapter VIII
    number of books lent and borrowed 110
Ireland, Northern. Report of the Departmental Committee on Libraries 47
Irish Central Library for Students 81

Joint Standing Committee on Library co-operation 59

Kenyon, Sir Frederic 49, 54
Kirby, S., Suggests central store for books in 1907 35

Lamb, J. P., On need for a central book store 145
Lending, how it is spread by means of a union catalogue 119–121
Librarians—
    brought together by regional systems 22
    future of co-operation in hands of 28

INDEX

London—
   co-operation between Borough libraries   97
   first inter-lending system in 1907   37
   library service in 1902, Sidney Webb on   34
   position of libraries in 1906, J. McKillop on   36
   public libraries union catalogue   125–130
   suggested central library in 1912   39

McKillop, J., On the position of London libraries in 1906   36
Mansbridge, Albert   49, 52
Mitchell, J. M.   48
   The public library system of Great Britain and Ireland   45

National Central Library—
   as a reserve store for little-used books   143
   first libraries to use and subscribe to   54
   Government grant to   56, 58
   how books in other libraries are traced   63–66
   its origin and development. Chapter III
   its place in the national system   Chapter IV
   policy of the Trustees   143
   recommendations of the Adult Education Committee, 1919   50
   recommendations of the Departmental Committee on Public Libraries   54–57
   recommendations of the Royal Commission on National Museums and Galleries   57
   reconstituted   58
   routine methods   67–72
   supply of bibliographical information   72
   type of book supplied   73
   type of book not supplied   61
   work of the Information Department   63
   work of the Library Department   61
National Committee on Regional Library Co-operation   98
Northern Ireland, a regional library system in   93

Outlier libraries Chapter V
    list of special 76-79
    number of volumes in 76
    union catalogue 130
Oxford—
    early attempts to compile a union catalogue 30
    inter-collegiate catalogue of books printed before 1641 134

Panizzi, Anthony. Suggests lending duplicates from British Museum in 1845 32
Panizzi Club 43
Philip, A. J.—
    A reference library for London 39
    organizes first inter-lending system in London in 1907 37
Pioneers of co-operation Chapter II
Pitt, S. A., Suggestions for co-operation 41
Pollard, A. W. 49
    The Central Library for Students 53
    Suggestions for co-operation in 1914 44
    Suggests a national lending library in 1913 41
Pollard, A. W., and Redgrave, G. R., *A short-title catalogue of books printed in England . . . 1475-1640* 138
Public libraries, persons who do not use 25
Public Libraries Committee, recommendations in reference to regional library systems 84

Reader, how he obtains a book 140-141
Recognized centre, advantage of using 23-25
Regional library systems Chapter VI
    bring librarians and authorities together 22
    co-operating libraries, number of 90
    history of their establishment 87-93
    how the systems function 93-99
    list of libraries not co-operating 91
    list of systems 89-90

INDEX 183

Regional library systems—*(continued)*
    Northern Ireland, position in 93
    number of books lent 92
    procedure for borrowing books 149–154
    recommendations of the Public Libraries Committee 84
    report of the County Libraries Section of the Library Association 85–87
    Scotland, position in 92
    Wales, early suggestions 83
    Yorkshire experiment 96
Royal Commission on National Museums and Galleries, recommendations of 57

Sale of books, increase in 21
Sandbach, F. E. 59
Scotland, a regional library system in 92
Scottish Central Library for Students 81
Scottish local history, union catalogue of 136
Special collections, libraries building up 147
Special outlier libraries, list of 76–79

Union catalogues Chapter IX
    additional uses for 124
    alternatives to 121–123
    Cambridge inter-collegiate catalogue 135
    catalogue of architectural drawings 136
    catalogue of outlier libraries 130
    catalogue of Scottish local history 136
    cost of material 130–131
    details of sheaf catalogues 131–133
    different forms of 125–134
    earliest printed 137
    how they enable all libraries to share in the lending 119–121
    information given in 125
    list of printed 172–176

Union catalogues—(*continued*)
    London public libraries union catalogue 125–130
    number of entries in 135
    number of single copies of books in 114–119
    Oxford, early suggestions 30
    Oxford inter-collegiate catalogue 134
    Panizzi Club's list of serials 43
    special card cabinets for 127
University libraries inter-lending system Chapter VII
    union catalogue of periodicals in 139

Wales, early suggestions for establishment of a regional library system 83
Webb, Sidney, On the library service of London in 1902 34
World list of scientific periodicals 139

Yorkshire Regional system working without a union catalogue 113

For Product Safety Concerns and Information please contact our EU representative GPSR@taylorandfrancis.com
Taylor & Francis Verlag GmbH, Kaufingerstraße 24, 80331 München, Germany

www.ingramcontent.com/pod-product-compliance
Lightning Source LLC
Chambersburg PA
CBHW061836300426
44115CB00013B/2407